Frank Hall was born in Wash Water, Hamps
young mother, Freda, died. His father, unabl
Frank and his sisters to Stonesfield in Oxfordshire. H
uncles and aunts and Freda's father, Grampy Bill, i
wells and transport was a strong pair of feet.

Frank's love of gardening inspired Aunt Edie to give him his first allotment and at the age of eleven he was expected to provide vegetables for the large family. After attending schools in Stonesfield and Charlbury, Frank's first job was in a Woodstock glove factory. Two years later, war was declared and as soon as he was old enough he joined the Home Guard.

In 1942 he was called up and became a soldier with the Oxford and Bucks Regiment and after training was told he would be joining the newly formed Sixth Airborne Division. He spent the war years as a driver in the Motor Transport Section, taking part in the Normandy Landings, the Ardennes fighting and the Rhine Crossing. After service in Palestine he left the army in 1947, with memories enough to last a lifetime.

Back in Stonesfield the winter was hard and Frank spent his first weeks digging in the snow to keep the village roads passable. He took work as a lorry driver for Oxfordshire Farmers and then a sand and gravel company but it was while he was helping out with a mobile fish and chip round that he met his future wife, Jean.

The couple lived in Bladon and had two children and, as Verger of St Martin's church, Frank's duties came to the fore with the burial of Sir Winston Churchill in 1965.

After seventeen years the Halls returned to Stonesfield. Frank, now a valued Sales Rep at the expanding Amey Roadstone Company, was soon involved in village activities including the Stonesfield Dance Club. He began to organise the Poppy Collections for the British Legion, a job he carried out until 2008, the year he finally gave up his allotment.

Rosemary Cleaver has lived in Stonesfield for seven years and has found it to be a warm, friendly village. She first met Frank when her husband took on an allotment and was fascinated by his ability to recall the past so clearly. Rosemary was not the first person to realise that these stories must not be lost and would make an intersting book, but she was lucky enough to be the one entrusted with the task.

She is a mother and grandmother and enjoys reading, writing and gardening. She spends much of her time working with her husband Mike in their shop in Burford.

Just Getting On With It

Frank's Story

As told by Rosemary Cleaver

The Wychwood Press

Our books may be ordered from bookshops or (post free) from
The Wychwood Press, Alder House, Market Street, Charlbury, OX7 3PH
01608 811969

e-mail: wychwood@joncarpenter.co.uk

Credit card orders should be phoned or faxed to 01689 870437
or 01608 811969

See our complete list at www.wychwoodpress.co.uk

First published in 2009 by
The Wychwood Press
an imprint of Jon Carpenter Publishing
Alder House, Market Street, Charlbury, Oxfordshire OX7 3PH

ISBN 978 1 902279 38 1

Preface

There's something about an allotment ... you feel it when you pass through the gate by the road. Whether it's walking into a place where you're suddenly surrounded by so many green, growing things; whether it's knowing that they'll come up year after year as inevitably as summer follows spring; whether it's being part of the battle to save cabbages and lettuce from caterpillars, pigeons, slugs and rabbits – and having to accept that sometimes you win and sometimes you lose; whether it's realising that you can't control your allotment but can only work with it ... there's just something there that quietens people, something that makes them stop and think and reminisce and talk.

There's a bench on our allotments and it belongs to a man named Frank Hall. From this bench came the story of a life at times a little more than ordinary...

I was delighted when Frank Hall agreed to tell me his story. Here is a man who has led a life worth hearing about. But although he can tell a good tale, it took some time to convince him that people really would be interested in his past if his memories were written down.

Once persuaded, Frank entered into the project with great enthusiasm, and I would like to thank him for all those meetings and for talking so freely about his experiences, although at times it must have been difficult. It was a privilege to learn so much about his family, his work and his part in the Second World War.

Frank has never been one to make a fuss and, if I asked how a person coped with some of the dreadful hardships of war, he would say to me, "Well, you just got on with it."

Thank you, Jean, for all the cups of tea and shortbread biscuits, and for putting us right when we were unsure of a name or date.

Thanks also go to Frank's sister, Marion, for reading the text and making some helpful suggestions and corrections.

I am especially grateful to Dale Morris who proof-read the book and sorted out all my grammatical errors and spelling mistakes. Also to her husband Richard who lent us some of the local photographs used in the book.

And last, but not least, I would like to thank my husband Mike, for it was he who sat on the allotment seat with Frank and finally persuaded him to let me write his story.

Rosemary Cleaver

Frank's mother, Freda Clarke (1913)

1

When Frank was born in 1923, his family lived in a cottage at The Mill in Wash Water, just outside Newbury on the Andover Road. The cottage, which stood a quarter of a mile from the main road, belonged to Jack Smith's farm in Burghclere where Frank's father, Percy Hall, was employed. Percy had been born and bred in this area and did not leave until war broke out.

Percy and his two brothers, Dan and Ted, had fought in the 1914-18 war along with their younger brother, Cecil, who was a regular soldier and PT instructor. Fortunately all four men survived the fighting and came home safely. Frank's father returned in November 1919. He had suffered from gas poisoning during the war and it had affected his eyesight.

As soon as he was discharged from the army he started attending St Dunstan's Eye Hospital in London every week. This was a long journey and despite the treatment he was being given there seemed to be no improvement. Fed up with the situation, one day Percy asked the surgeon to be honest with him about his condition. He was told that his eyesight would gradually deteriorate and that he would eventually go blind.

"Well, in that case," said the young man, "It seems to me that I'm wasting your time and you're wasting mine so I don't think I'll come any more."

So the visits to the hospital ceased and Frank's father accepted the gradual loss of vision as inevitable.

While he was in the Royal Army Service Corps he had been sent to Stonesfield in Oxfordshire, a village on the edge of the Cotswold Hills to the northwest of Oxford and close to Woodstock with its famous palace of Blenheim. Stonesfield had had a mining industry for three hundred years, producing the beautiful roofing slates which grace so many Cotswold houses and Oxford colleges. The last slate was mined in 1911 and by the time of the First World War most people in the village worked in farming or glove-making. Percy spent some time baling hay in the fields near Stonesfield for the military horses and it was here that he met his future wife, Freda Clarke, who lived with her parents in the village. After the war Percy and Freda married and moved down to his home area of Wash Water. Here, he went to work on the farm and the young couple soon started their family.

Emma, always known as Emmie, was born first in the little cottage. Sixteen months later, during a spell of severe wintry weather, the snow lay so deep that it reached the tops of the hedges. On a day when the temperature was well below freezing Mrs Hall sent her husband to fetch the midwife to help with her second birth. Percy had to walk a mile to the woman's house and when he returned he said the snow was frozen so hard that he could walk straight over the hedgerows without sinking. But the midwife arrived and later that day, February 19th, Frank made his entrance into the world. He weighed just three pounds and everyone wondered if he would survive. But with his mother's care he began to thrive and grew up well and strong.

As well as mother and father and his sister, the other important member of Frank's family was a sheep dog. This dog, as well as working on the farm, played with the two children and the three of them had some jolly times together. Their father had made a little truck with shafts attached and fixed a pair of old pram wheels onto it. Frank and Emmie took turns to sit in this truck and to travel in style down to the main road and back, the dog between the shafts, happy to trot up and down time and time again with the other child running behind.

After a while the farmer needed the cottage for his daughter and the Hall family moved onto the farm at Burghclere for two years. By the time Frank was five years old they had moved again, this time to a house called Somersby, a redbrick house on the edge of Newtown, just off the old A34 past Sandleford Priory. Frank's next sister, Marion, was born on New Year's Day, 1928, soon after they arrived. It was another hard winter and her father was out clearing snow when she was born. He always joked, "If I'd been home when you arrived I might have sent you back!"

By now, it was time for Frank to start school and he attended Burghclere school, which took children from many of the villages south of Newbury. The school bus passed the front door, but the road was

The Swan public house, near Newtown (1935)

deemed too narrow for it to stop (a 1928 traffic hazard) so, for almost five years, the children walked a quarter of a mile to the Swan public house, from where the bus took them to Burghclere.

Frank was taught by Miss Cox, the baker's daughter. The school had a playing field where the pupils played sports and games and this was where Frank had one of those little accidents that used to happen frequently before the days of protective clothing. He was wicket keeping during a match when the young batsman's rather old, splintery cricket bat came swinging up behind and clouted Frank on the side of the face. It was a nasty cut so Miss Cox accompanied him down to the doctor's surgery.

The old doctor was shortly due to retire and was training a younger man to take over. He decided that Frank needed a couple of stitches and offered to do the job there and then. But Miss Cox considered for a minute, looked at his fading eyes and shaky hands, and said, "No thank you, we'll wait for Dr Kendle." Probably a wise decision.

Mr Hall had a big garden and grew all the vegetables a family could need. For other food the market at Newbury was a good place to go and on a Saturday afternoon father, mother and the children would put on their coats and walk into the town. Stallholders were thinking of packing up by now and were only too happy to get rid of their goods

Freda with her father, George and Edie (1920)

at this time of day. You could get a real bargain in the late afternoon: a big piece of bacon for 6d and a whole stack of bananas for just a few pence.

Frank's mother was a small, dainty woman. The home and children kept her very busy but she was keen to learn to ride a bicycle. Percy tried to teach her, but it was not too successful and Freda seemed to spend much of the time sitting on the bike and leaning against the wall shaking with laughter. Although she enjoyed life, her health was never good and sometimes Frank and Emmie were asked to enter the Swan by the back door to pick up a Guinness which she hoped would build her up. But by the time the children's mother became pregnant again in 1932 her heart was weakened. Emmie, who was twelve by this time, had been sent to live with her grandfather and the family at Stonesfield because it was felt that four children would be too much for her mother. Mary was born on November 27th and Freda was not very well.

When the baby was ten weeks old the children's mother passed away. She was just thirty-five years old. Frank's grief-stricken father did not know what would happen to his family now. He could not work and look after three children at the same time. There was talk of sending them to the nearest Dr Barnardo's home. Nobody wanted this to happen, least of all their grandfather in Stonesfield. So he and Freda's brother and sister offered to take Frank, Marion and baby Mary and bring them up as best they could, along with Emmie. Sadly, there was no room for their father Percy who had to stay behind. But he had a very good friend in Newtown who kindly offered him lodgings which he accepted so he could continue to work.

On February 4th 1933 the children left Somersby. Two days later Freda's body was brought to Stonesfield and buried in the churchyard.

2

Grampy and Granny Clarke had been living in Timberyard in Stonesfield in half of a pair of cottages. After his wife's early death Grampy Bill had remained there with his two unmarried children, George and Edie. In the other part of the house lived Frank's Great-uncle Frank, a soldier who had been the only man from the village to fight in the Boer War, and Great-aunt Annie whose father had worked in the Stonesfield slate pits. Granny Clarke had died when George was ten years old and Annie, who used to teach at Stonesfield school, had looked after George. (Now, at ten, Frank had lost his mother so history repeated itself.)

George had been a bright boy when he was young but full of mischief and often in trouble at school. In fact one day he asked Aunt Annie if the headmaster, Mr Stammers, was well. When Auntie Annie said that yes, he was and wanted to know why George had asked, he said, "Well, I just wondered because I haven't had the cane today."

In George's class was a boy called Harry Oliver. One day, the teacher chose Harry to tell him the names of the four Channel Islands and said he could have a few minutes to think about it. George, always clever but ready to play a trick most of the time, passed forward the answer on a piece of paper. The schoolmaster looked at Harry and said, "Have you thought about it then, Oliver?"

Harry looked at his piece of paper and answered, "Yes Sir – Jersey, Guernsey, Sleeve Waistcoat and Slop."

The master asked who had told Harry this but a glance behind from the boy and the look on George's face left him in no doubt. Oliver and Clarke were hauled to the front of the class and given two on each hand, George for writing and Harry for cheating.

George had picked up a jackdaw when it was young and somehow he had taught it to speak. This bird was devoted to him and liked to accompany him whenever it could, often causing a bit of a commotion. Occasionally when the children were being marched round the school playground the bird would sit on the wall and watch. Unfortunately, it could also mimic the teacher and call out 'Halt!' to the class. This was usually followed by, "Clarke! Take that bird home."

When George went to church he needed to make sure that the door to the vestry was closed. Otherwise the jackdaw would walk in quietly and then start calling, to the amusement of the younger members of the congregation and annoyance of the vicar,

"Where's George?"

As well as teaching at school, Aunt Annie used to work at home sewing gloves. Glove-making was an important industry in Woodstock and at that time there were four glove factories in the town and several in Charlbury. All had outworkers who could earn 8d a pair for quality hand-sown seams. This fell to 4d if the woman used a sewing machine. Annie worked near the window to get the best light and the jackdaw liked to watch her. He used to 'help' by picking up all the odds and ends of thread she'd cut and put them into little piles. But if she left her needle about while she went to tend to something in the kitchen she would find it and the bird both gone and have to find another.

Although George spent a good part of his schooldays having fun he had no trouble in making progress with his lessons and by the time he'd grown up he had quite a reputation as an educated man and was a butcher by trade. When Frank came to live with him his handwriting and literary talents were well known and quite a number of people in the village came to George when they wanted a letter written.

And so a new life began for Frank and his sisters. But Stonesfield was not completely strange to the children. Sometimes they had travelled here with their parents by taking the train to Woodstock, Frank guiding his father by the hand so that Percy's failing sight would not cause him to bump into people.

Frank, Marion and Mary arrived in Stonesfield to find six people in the house already. As well as their sister Emmie, there were five grown-ups so a bit of re-organisation was needed to fit in the children as well. There were four bedrooms – two on the first floor and two attic rooms. Little Mary slept in a cot in her great-aunt's bedroom, Emmie shared a room with Auntie Edie and Frank was put in one of the attic bedrooms. However, Marion did not stay with the others but moved in to the house next door. The couple living here were Auntie Tilly and Uncle Alf Hopkins who were the niece and nephew of Great-aunt Annie. There was some talk of Frank joining them too but he had settled in with Grampy Bill and Edie and George.

Downstairs, the Clarke's house was not very large for this number of people. The living room had to double as a dining room and the kitchen was quite small. Outside the kitchen was a little porch with a wooden bench. A large black pot hung over the kitchen fireplace so that vegetables and meat could be thrown in to bubble away, ready for the next meal. Coal was stored in the kitchen because the fire had to be kept alight all the time, for boiling water and cooking. Wood came from Stockey Bottom where Frank and the other children were sent to pick up fallen branches and twigs from the trees for burning. Great-uncle Frank and Great-aunt Annie had a little fire and a cooking range in their room. Uncle Frank worked as a shepherd at Westfield Farm in Combe. He used to walk home along the river and across the allotments.

As soon as Annie saw him striding between the rows of vegetables she would put the kettle on. Sitting by the fire, listening to the old tin kettle singing, Uncle Frank would take a slice of bread and pierce it with his toasting fork. Then, holding it over the glowing coals he waited until it was golden brown and soon there was toast for tea.

One day, as Annie looked through the window, she saw her husband carrying something across his shoulders. Outside, he showed her a walnut sapling that he had brought from Westfield Farm. He planted it near the wall that separated the garden from the allotments and slowly it grew into the strong, graceful tree that looks down on the plots today.

The kitchen sink was only small but it was in constant use although there was no running water in the village. The family drew their water

The River Evenlode in 1933

from a well which was also used by the Adams and Scarrott families who lived a little way down the hill in cottages overlooking Stockey Bottom. Mr Adams and Mr Scarrott had the right of way over a footpath running past the front of the Clarkes' and Hopkins' cottages to the well, which served the four households. Water from this well was clear and fresh for drinking but had to be used for cooking, bathing, cleaning and washing too. Monday was always washing day. To save the precious well water Frank was often sent down to the River Evenlode wearing a wooden yoke from which hung two buckets. He filled these from the river and brought them back up the hill so that there could be plenty of water for the following day's wash. By doing this and making sure the well was covered and not over-used there was a constant supply of fresh water.

Grampy Bill had dug wells in Stonesfield for many years. As the well got deeper he would be lowered down and pass up bucket after bucket of earth and rocks. In the grounds of Stonesfield Manor he had to dig one hundred feet down before he found water and he said that when he looked up at the sky, from the bottom of a hole that deep, he could even see stars in the daytime.

Bill worked on the Ditchley Park estate and walked there and back every day, a distance of at least three miles. He was also the Sexton at the church and sometimes Frank helped his grandfather when he dug the graves. This was hard work because the land in Stonesfield, as its name suggests, has always been full of stones. Graves were dug completely by hand, their sides beautifully vertical and following the shape of the coffin to perfection. To achieve this Grampy Bill had to split straight through stones, using an iron bar to tap the stone and listen for its weak point before breaking it. A standard grave was five feet deep but a double would need to be seven and at this depth there were often huge slabs of rock like tables.

It was a long job and meant taking time off from Ditchley Park. So that he would not lose more than one day's pay, Bill needed to start digging at six in the morning for a funeral taking place that same afternoon. After a grave had been dug the stone that had been removed could amount to twelve or thirteen wheelbarrow-loads. Frank liked to help his grandfather take it to the Cross and tip it on the ground on the western side. All the farmers knew about this heap of rock and sooner or later they would come along with a horse and cart and pick up as much as they needed. Most of the stone was tipped into field gateways to make the muddy entrances less of a problem in wet weather.

3

Frank and Marion started attending their new school in Stonesfield. Frank was there for a year before he moved up to the secondary school at Spendlove, just a few miles away in Charlbury. He did, however, manage to get his name in the school punishment book more than once before he left – there was one entry for 'dissobedience' and another rather more interesting one for 'splashing ink on girls' clean dresses'.

Frank enjoyed Charlbury school and travelled every day with his friend Don Parsons who lived up by the village cross. School buses were provided for children from the surrounding villages by a Charlbury firm called Morrison's who had a bus station in Market

Street. Best behaviour was required on the school bus, particularly as Mr Watts, who taught science and woodwork, lived in Stonesfield and so travelled on the bus with the pupils. If anyone spoke too loudly or wriggled about too much Mr Watts would immediately call to the driver, "Mr Timms, stop the bus!" And to the troublemaker: "You – see me at nine in the morning!"

The offending child had to get off the bus. This often meant a walk of a mile or two, perhaps in bad weather. And when the parents found out why their son or daughter was late there could well be a good hiding in addition to being thoroughly wet and cold. In those times teachers were very important members of the community and always kept a careful eye on their pupils' behaviour out of school hours. If a child was seen so much as climbing over a gate or wall it would be no surprise to him or her to be called out of class the following day.

Children could buy school dinners but Frank and Don took sandwiches for their lunch every day. The bus used to pick up the boys outside Stonesfield school and while they waited for it to arrive they would often hang their bags on the gatepost. Sometimes though, they were so wrapped up in their conversation that the bags were forgotten and this meant a whole day at school without food – unless the boys could scrounge a morsel off someone else. Luckily, the bags would still be on the gatepost when the pupils returned and empty tummies could be satisfied in no time between the bus stop and home.

Frank's father Percy was a great gardener and his son inherited his Dad's love of the soil and being outdoors. Don Parsons enjoyed the same things and so the pair were very keen on working the patch of garden they shared at Charlbury school. They were taught by a Mr Bill Campbell who was a great encouragement to both boys. Every Monday morning the headmaster would walk round inspecting the pupils' patches and decide which garden looked the most attractive and well-cared for. Then, the result was announced at the morning assembly and nine times out of ten the winners were 'Frank Hall and Don Parsons'. There was no prize but to a couple of keen gardeners the honour of being mentioned and of pleasing Mr Campbell was enough.

In 1934 Stonesfield village had a great many allotments. Grampy Clarke's house was surrounded by the Churchfields allotments which stretched from Brook Lane to the old Methodist chapel and back to

Stockey Bottom. All this land was owned by the church. Aunt Edie had heard about Frank's successes with the school garden and thought it would be good if the family could benefit a bit from his talents. She came up with an excellent plan and one day when Frank came home from school she said,

"Ah Frank – I've got something for you."

"Oh great," said Frank. "What is it?"

Auntie walked him up to the top of the garden and said, "See that allotment there? Well, it was going spare and I've been up to see the Rector and it's yours."

So, at the age of eleven, Frank had the new responsibility of providing vegetables for the family. Every day, weather permitting, he would come home from school and spend two hours digging, planting, weeding and harvesting. He was soon pleased to be joined on the allotments by Don. Don's father worked an allotment near Brook Lane and before too long managed to get a plot for his son. The boys' common interest kept them both very busy; the only difference between them being that Frank gave his produce to the family but Don managed to sell most of his.

The villagers all knew each other and because people walked everywhere there was plenty of time to note exactly who was growing what in their gardens. Almost everyone grew their own vegetables but it was possible to buy all the other things a family would need without leaving Stonesfield. Uncle George worked in Mrs Tidmarsh's butcher's shop which was not far from the house. The beef cattle came from Combe, the next village, and sometimes Frank helped bring the animals across from here to the slaughter house which stood behind the shop. Milk and eggs were bought from Teddy Griffin at Charity Farm, near the Cross, or any of the farmers in the village, like Bernard Hunt, Walter Austin or Wilf Barrett.

The nearest farm to Frank's family was Mr Paulin's, a smallholding in Churchfields. In the 1930s Churchfields was still a cobbled road and the children could hear the farmer's cows' or ponies' hooves as they clattered along towards Brook Lane. Here, Mr Paulin would leave the cows to make their own way down to the field, knowing that the next time he stood at the top of the lane and called they would come lumbering back. In the winter the farmer's hurricane lamp was a lonely

Joseph Hunt's threshing engines (1936)

light as it bobbed along Churchfields.

At the top of Church Street, near the Cross, was Mrs Shearer's grocery store and on the other side of the Cross was a shop belonging to Uncle Alf. He sold useful items like black lead for the grate, boot polish, paraffin for the lamps and foodstuffs like cocoa and sugar. Radio sets ran on batteries and people could leave their accumulators with Uncle Alf for recharging. Across the road stood the Black Head public house and a short walk to the corner led to Eric Hanks, the baker.

Opposite Hanks's Corner was an engine yard. Here, Joseph Hunt kept two fine steam-driven threshing team engines, one named 'Bonus' and the other 'Flying Rose'. These were hired out to the farmers at harvest time along with their drivers, Mr Scarrott (the Clarkes' neighbour) and Mr Woodley. Other drivers in the village acted as carriers; Ken and Vic Griffin would travel in the Oxford direction and Billy Oliver regularly took a group of women to work on a farm at Kingston Bagpuize.

Stonesfield also had its builders in Phil and Fred Davies and Arthur and George Griffin. It boasted seven plasterers: Jack and Ern Davies, Bert and Jo Hunt, Harold Hall, Wilf Griffin and Simmy Oliver. And next door to Arthur and George the builders, towards the bottom end of Churchfields, lived the wheelwright and undertaker, Charles Dore.

4

Everyone in the village seemed to visit Charlie Dore's place. He and Mrs Dore were village 'characters'. Small in stature, and only needing a size four shoe, Charlie wore a long smock which brushed the ground and a trilby hat. Mrs Dore was also tiny, although well-known for having larger feet than her husband, and never seen without her warm woollen hat pulled well down onto her head. When war broke out in 1939 the villagers were issued with gas masks. Everyone had to go to the school for a fitting and then they were given their mask in its brown cardboard box. But there was one person in Stonesfield who had to go without, and that was Charlie Dore. Despite his smallness, Charlie had the misfortune of having such a long chin that no gas mask could be found to fit him.

Charlie was a jack-of-all-trades who could mend cars and restore bicycles, to name but two of his talents. Frank bought his first bicycle from him. Charlie had a Morris Oxford that he used as a taxi and a pump from which he sold petrol. He would set the needle to the one gallon mark on the dial and then wind the handle round until the needle pointed to '0'. If anyone needed more than a gallon of petrol he would repeat the process. In later years, when television came to the village, some people began to approach Charlie for help with the considerable cost of buying one of these exciting new devices. He did not own a set himself but when someone remarked on this, he let it be known that "half of 'em in the village belongs to me".

At the front of Charlie's cottage was a tin shed. There was a large padlock on the door of the shed because it housed various useful items like torches, which were for sale. One day Frank needed a battery for his torch so he went down to the Dore's and knocked. Batteries were not kept in the shed but in the house and Mrs Dore went to search for one. As usual, Frank waited outside because it was not the couple's practice to ask people in. On her return she said to Frank, "Frank, I think we're out of new batteries but I've taken this one out of my torch and you can have it half price."

Charlie was responsible for most of the funerals in Stonesfield and established his own very high standards when it came to coffins and graves. He would visit the house of the person who had died and measure up the body so that he could make the coffin a perfect fit, cutting strips of wood and clamping them to follow the angle of the shoulders. For something so carefully crafted Charlie demanded no less precision when it came to the hole it was going to rest in. He would give Grampy Bill and Uncle John the measurements they were to work to, allowing a gap of precisely two inches all around the coffin – no more, no less. But the gravediggers had high standards too and there was never a problem when the coffin was lowered.

Walk a little way along Churchfields and there was a lane, not far from Charlie's place. This was where Mr and Mrs Dore decided to build a smart new bungalow for their retirement. Charlie was very pleased with it, having made sure it was all constructed to his own specifications. Although the neighbours thought it was a very fine bungalow they noticed that the wall, which ran all round the boundary of his garden, was not so attractive - the plain side being on the outside; the decorative side hidden from view. When one fellow, thinking the builders had placed the blocks the wrong way round, dared to mention this Charlie said, "Yes – that's why it's done. So I can look out the window and look at 'em - not for you to look at as you go walking past!" Although they had hoped to live in the bungalow the Dores never moved in. Ill health forced them to rent it to a family friend and the old couple remained at what is now Apple Tree Cottage for the rest of their days.

While it was possible to buy all their day-to-day provisions in Stonesfield, sometimes it was necessary for the villagers to walk to one of the nearby towns for other services. Like most people in Stonesfield, Frank's family went to Charlbury if they needed to see a doctor. This meant a walk or cycle ride of a few miles to Dr Crowley's surgery in Station Road. Luckily, the family were usually very healthy. But if anyone in the village was too ill to make the journey to Charlbury, Dr Crowley would come over to Stonesfield in his chauffeur-driven car to see the patient. Mrs Pratley from Combe Road could always be relied upon to cycle over to Charlbury to pick up their prescriptions and medicines.

When Grampy Bill was still alive he used to walk Frank along the old field paths to Charlbury on a Saturday morning to get his hair cut. After his grandfather had died Frank had his hair trimmed nearer home. Two men from the village, Joe Hunt and George Scarrott, were willing to have a go with a pair of scissors if people were prepared to take a chance on the outcome, but neither had been trained as barbers. Frank, who was concerned for his appearance, preferred to go to Mr Bedford, the barber from Woodstock. Mr Bedford visited Stonesfield every Thursday. One week he would have his 'appointments' but on alternate weeks he paid Mr Parsons of The Ridings for the use of his living room. Here, Frank and the other boys waited for a sixpenny haircut. They always had plenty of time but the men were keen to get back to work. Occasionally one of them would say, "You in a hurry, Frank?" When Frank said that no, he wasn't really, the man would pay him a penny for his place in the queue. That meant that as soon as the haircutting was done Frank and any of his friends who had struck lucky could go straight down to the post office in Boot Street where Miss Osborne, the postmistress, also sold sweets. So a haircut could often mean a few Bulls' Eyes as well.

Miss Osborne was in a position to know quite a lot about most people in the village and she could easily recognise everyone's handwriting. One day, Frank's auntie gave him a letter to post, along with the money to buy a stamp. Messing about on the way and coming across a few friends made the boy forget the time. When Frank got to the post office it was closed. Oh dear, now what was he going to do? He thought for a minute and decided there was only one thing for it; he popped the letter into the box, posted the tuppence ha'penny after it and hoped for the best. It worked. Next time Frank went into the post office Miss Osborne said, "Oh, I got your letter Frank and the money, so I put a stamp on for you."

So although it was nigh on impossible to conduct any business in private, sometimes this could be quite advantageous.

Occasionally the children bought a toy from the post office. Frank's friend, Doug Woodley, was lucky enough to have some money for a little wooden car. He was very pleased with it and tied a piece of string onto the front. The two boys pulled the car all around the village. This was good fun and so they did it again. However, after the second trip Doug decided that he was rather bored with the car and would like his

The Boot Street post office(1926)

money back. So he cleaned up the wheels, hoped Miss Osborne would not see any scratches and said to her, "My Mum says I can't have this car. Can I change it for some sweets?"

Miss Osborne obliged.

Mr Bedford the barber was not the only person to come over from Woodstock for trade. Every Saturday, early in the morning, a man would leave Woodstock on foot, laden with two trays and two baskets. These were overflowing with faggots and hogs' puddings to sell to the people of Stonesfield. By 9 o'clock his trays were empty and he caught the bus back to Woodstock. Other traders came to the village - Carlo's sold fish and chips and monkeynuts from a van and Frost's and Marriot's brought coal. Being in a village did not mean isolation in the 1930s.

5

The family made up part of the congregation at the parish church of St James the Great. Frank walked up to the church three times on Sundays: once for morning service; then for Sunday School in the afternoon, where the children had to learn the Collect for the next week;

and back again for Evensong at 6 o'clock. Digging the allotment – or any other kind of work - was not allowed on a Sunday. Besides, with most of the day taken up with church attendance there was no time for anything else, except perhaps a walk. Playing was forbidden, especially with children in their best clothes.

Uncle Alf was the church organist. The organ had a foot pedal for pumping in air and it was easier for the person playing the instrument if someone else operated this. Uncle Alf asked Frank to do the job and Frank agreed. He pumped the organ for his uncle from the age of eleven until he left the village to join the army. There was a weight hanging down the side of the organ; the position of this weight told the organist how much air pressure he'd got. On the days of the great festivals such as Harvest and Easter Alf wanted a really powerful blast from the pipes, saying, "You'll have to pump quick today, boy!"

Uncle Alf's father, known to Frank as Uncle John, was the verger and churchwarden at St. James's, carrying the cross at the front of the procession on festival days. Sometimes the St. James's church banner would also be needed and this was usually carried by Frank. Uncle John was very busy with church matters, another of his jobs being to help Grampy Bill when a grave needed to be dug. His son followed in his footsteps because not only was Alf the church organist but he was a bell ringer and captain of the church tower.

Frank was happy at the church and it was not long before Alf asked him if he would like to start ringing. His nephew was keen to learn this new skill and started off with enthusiasm. But bellringing was not easy and Alf turned out to be a hard taskmaster. Before long Frank was losing interest and confided in Aunt Annie. She went up to Alf's shop one day before bell practice and said, "Frank says he's not coming bell-ringing any more – it's too hard."

Alf replied sharply, "You make sure he gets up there!"

So that was that. Frank had no choice but to work hard and learn all the intricacies of bellringing: how to hold the rope with its 'sally' and 'tag's end'; how to pull a little harder with every effort until the bell was upside down; how to work with the slides and stays so that the bell hung in the balance, neither down nor up. Bells seemed to have minds of their own and the only thing they wanted to do was to come swinging down, leaving the ringer with a useless, slack rope.

The parish church (1930s)

Eventually, after about twelve months, Frank was beginning to feel that at last he was controlling the bell, rather than the other way round. He had learned the valuable lesson: The only way to ring a bell Down was to keep it Up.

Church services and a day off work were the only things that made Christmas Day different from any other. There was no stocking for the children but Uncle George would bring home a nice piece of beef from the shop for dinner. The family never had a holiday and outings were rare but the children always found ways to entertain and interest themselves in the village.

The boys enjoyed watching the men's football team as they practised. They would stand behind the goal posts and wait for one of the players to kick the ball wide of the goal. Then the first boy to get to the ball could kick it back onto the pitch.

During the summer the men turned to cricket and the team practised in the warm, light evenings in Ken Griffin's field up on the Ridings. The field sloped considerably down towards the valley so the ball would gather speed as it disappeared towards the bottom. The men used to tell the boys that if they ran after the ball and brought it back they could have a go at batting later. Frank and Don and the others were very keen on trying out their skills with the bat and duly spent most of the evening running up and down the field. Then, about five or ten minutes before the end of the evening one of the cricketers would call: "Come on, you boys! You can have a bat now."

About six balls would be bowled and then someone would say, "Oh dear, it's too dark now. Come tomorrow and you can have another go."

So, always hopeful, the boys would turn up again the following evening. But the same thing happened every time.

Boys and girls played with whips and tops and ran around the

The Ridings, Stonesfield (1900)

Stonesfield streets with iron hoops. Holding an iron bar with a hook on the end, the child could guide the hoop in the right direction, working up to quite a speed.

Frank and his friends liked to go down to the river to do a bit of fishing. They could make a rod by tying a piece of string round a hazelnut stick, because they were nice and straight and whippy, and hooking a bent pin onto the end of the string. Very few, if any, fish were caught but the fun was in the planning, watching and waiting and just being together. Occasionally they would see other fishermen and go have a look at them in action.

The river was quite rich in crayfish and Walter Austin, the farmer from High Street, liked to catch them. He would catch a lot of these strange little creatures and take them home to be plunged, still alive, into a pot of boiling water. When they were cooked the crayfish could be pulled open and small pieces of meat found in the body region and the claws. The boys never caught them for themselves but if they were playing around Stony Bridge in the evenings they liked to lift the stones until they came across a crayfish hiding there. Then they would set it free and watch it waddle away to find another dark, wet place away from boys and other predators.

It was a good and happy life for Frank and his sisters, but he was growing up fast and all too soon the time came when he had to leave childish things behind and step into the adult world.

6

In 1937, at the age of fourteen, Frank left Charlbury school and went to work in Dent's glove factory in Back Lane at Woodstock. This factory belonged to Dent's of Worcester and along with the other three factories in the town – Pullman's, Lance Clothier's and Atherton and Clothier's – produced high quality leather gloves with various linings from cloth to rabbit's fur. As well as these four factories there was another firm producing cricket gloves. The five establishments ensured a high rate of employment in the area. Crates of leather skins came by train from Kidlington into Woodstock station and these would be collected by a man with a horse and trolley, who then delivered them to all the factories.

There were about forty people employed in Dent's factory. Eight to twelve people worked in the cutting room and about the same number of girls operated the sewing machines. After they were sewn up, the gloves were passed to a man who was skilled in stretching them over a brass hand and pulling them into shape. Then they would be passed to the packing room to be parcelled up and dispatched by the office.

In the cutting room the skins were stretched in all directions and the right and left hand glove patterns placed on the leather. When the men had finished cutting from a skin, the left over pieces were sent to Frank and the three others who worked in the slitting room. This room produced the six narrow strips of leather called fourchettes which joined the front and back sections of the glove fingers. The leather was put into a press and when a handle was pulled down the sharp edges of the shaped metal section came down, stamping out the fourchette. Great care was needed to make sure that the main parts of a pair of gloves, as well as all the fourchettes, were perfectly matching in colour and texture. Apart from keeping the floor swept, Frank worked on the press for most of the day.

During the week, work started at eight in the morning and finished at half-past five in the evening. On Saturdays the factory closed at half-past twelve, in time for lunch. Frank earned 7/6d a week and gave all but 6d to Aunt Edie. He used to cycle to Woodstock and back with Millie Oliver who also worked in the factory. Millie often brought back parcels of gloves ready for sewing to give to her neighbours who were outworkers. It suited many women from the surrounding villages to work at home for the factories in Woodstock and Charlbury. Gloves were delivered to, and collected from, Bladon, Glympton and Kiddington, Finstock, Fawler and Spelsbury as well as Stonesfield.

When Frank had been working at the factory for three months the job of boilerman was offered to him. The boiler needed to be lit at seven every morning so that the factory would be comfortable and the water hot by eight o'clock. This meant leaving home at six-thirty in the morning but since the job brought with it an extra 2/- a week Frank decided he would put up with the dark, cold ride to Woodstock.

He stayed at Dent's for eighteen months but then thought he would like to work outdoors. An opportunity came up at Bridewell Farm, a few miles away at North Leigh and within easy cycling distance. The farm was owned by two sisters, the Misses Lamb. On September 3rd, in 1939, Frank was working on the farm here when news of the war with Germany quickly spread throughout the countryside.

Soon after the outbreak of war, towns and villages were encouraged to form their own battalions of the LDV: Local Defence Volunteers, later to be renamed the Home Guard. In Stonesfield the branch HQ was in a shepherd's hut; a square wooden structure on four wheels. Farmers were able to move these huts around so that the shepherds could be near the sheep during lambing. The LDV hut belonged to Bernard Hunt of Woodleys farm and he drew it up into a field, belonging to the Crown pub, on the Woodstock Road.

The Stonesfield men and boys wanted to do their bit for the war effort. ARP Wardens appeared and walked around the village checking that buildings were all blacked out at night. Uncle George became a Special Constable and was under the guidance of Nobby Clarke, the village bobby, also based in Woodstock Road. In May 1940 Frank was listening to the radio one evening when he heard about the new Local Defence Volunteers and realised that at seventeen he would be allowed to join them. He told Aunt Edie what he was thinking and, after he had eaten his tea, went up to Nobby Clarke's house and rang the doorbell. The door was answered by Mr Watts, Frank's old teacher, who looked at him and said, "What are you doing up here, Frank?"

Frank told him he had come to join the LDV, to which Mr Watts replied, "Well done for you – I've just joined so you're the second one."

So Frank went inside, saw Nobby and signed on the dotted line, to become one of the Stonesfield Local Defence Volunteers or the LDV, soon to be known affectionately by its members as 'Look, Duck and Vanish'. Being a man of some local standing, Mr Watts was made the commanding officer. He was a talented man with varied interests, one being photography, and had his own darkroom in his cottage in High Street. His interest in guns came in very useful when he was in charge of the LDV and he equipped sixteen of the men with weapons from his own collection. Eventually the Home Guard were issued with rifles but at this stage men in other villages and towns were practising their weapons drill with sticks.

Frank in his LDV uniform, May 1940

The LDV kept watch from the shepherd's hut every night, from six in the evening until six the following morning. Don Parsons had also joined up and the two young men were usually on guard together. A night watch needed three pairs of men, each pair being on duty for two two-hour stints. Frank and Don preferred six till eight in the evening followed by midnight till 2 o'clock because they could still get in a reasonable amount of sleep before morning. On Sunday mornings the pair often slept on until 9 or 10 o'clock, waking up in the hut to find the fire dead and the other volunteers long gone. If there was an air raid warning the wardens would come into the hut as well and a good game of cards soon started. Later, in the clear, quiet, still night German bombers could be heard moaning overhead although nothing could be seen. The following morning would bring news that Coventry had been raided again.

Despite the seriousness of their work there were plenty of good laughs from the LDV chaps as they huddled round the fire. War, despite its horror, brought out the best in people, forcing them together in the comradeship that memories are made of. As well as companionship and a sense of doing his duty there was another benefit for Frank. His LDV sergeant, Clarrie Fowler's father, had been in the Ox and Bucks regiment during the First World War and gave the young volunteer an excellent grounding in the drill used by the regiment. Frank was in the LDV and then Home Guard for eighteen months before he was called up and this training was to be very useful when he himself joined the Ox and Bucks later on.

7

Frank, whilst working at Bridewell Farm, was offered a job paying rather higher wages. A position as labourer came up with the two plasterers, Bert and Jo Hunt, so he left the fields and went back indoors. The Hunts used to work on many of the older cottages, repairing and replacing the original lath and plaster finishes. At the time of Frank's employment they were working regularly for Hill Brothers of Eynsham, one of the bigger building firms in the area. The firm was situated in Witney Road, Eynsham and Frank helped Bert and Joe with the plastering of the new houses that Hill's were building all along this road in 1940.

After his work with the Hunts, Frank was employed by Frost's, the coal merchant. George Franklin from Stonesfield was a manager with this firm and his two sons, Reg and Peter, used to work for their father. Frost's main office was in Witney, near the Buttercross. Witney station was sizeable and very busy with goods traffic constantly coming in and it was here that B.T. Frost had their largest depot. All the vehicles were kept painted up and maintained at the station depot before being loaded up with coal. The firm also had smaller depots at Long Hanborough, Charlbury and Bampton stations and further afield in Brackley and Chipping Norton.

About 500 tons of coal were delivered to the mansion at Ditchley Park each year. The park was owned by Ronald Tree, and to keep his huge house warm very small nuggets of coal called beans were fed into a large hopper. At the bottom of the hopper was a constantly turning wheel that fed the beans to the boilers. Reg, who drove the lorry, and Frank used to deliver house coal, as well as the beans, to the mansion where a wing of the building had been commandeered by the government for wartime planning. On one visit Frank met Anthony Eden here. Although the surroundings were very grand the coal was tipped straight onto the floor of one of the rooms. The men also delivered to Model Farm on the estate, the farm managers' houses and the estate lodges. After the weekly delivery Reg would let his mate have a go at driving the empty lorry along the back roads towards Stonesfield where the lorry was kept in the yard by the side of Mrs Shearer's shop. Quite soon Frank became a confident driver.

During the war coal, used by every household and all the factories, was eventually in short supply. The firm had to 'rob Peter to pay Paul' and find supplies from wherever they could to keep their customers happy. One of the places Reg and Frank would drive to was the canal wharf in Oxford where they unloaded coal brought down from Coventry by barge. Frank enjoyed his work but he knew that quite soon the call would come for him to join the army and leave home. At regular intervals an announcement was made on the radio by the BBC telling all men who had reached the age of eighteen and a half years that they must register at their nearest recruiting centre.

On a Saturday in December 1941 Frank went into the centre in St Giles in Oxford to enlist. After his own experiences in the army his father had always told him to choose the RAF for an easier life. So when the recruiting officer asked him which service he would like to join the hopeful young man answered, "The RAF."

The officer looked up and said, "No vacancies."

"The Royal Navy."

"No vacancies."

"What about The Guards?"

"No vacancies – Oxford and Bucks."

The Ox and Bucks no doubt had told the recruiting office that they needed a couple of hundred men and it was the St Giles' job to make sure they got them. In the evening the *Oxford Mail* published its usual report about the numbers registering that day and said that they had been able to choose their service. All that remained for Frank was to wait for the call.

One morning he walked up to the Cross and met George Franklin near the lorry.

"I shall be finishing on Friday," said Frank, "because I've got my calling up papers."

George told him that he could probably get the call-up deferred for a bit, but Frank said, "No thank you, if I've got to go I'll go now and get it done with."

On the morning of January 29th 1942, Frank left the village with Uncle George who dropped him off at Combe Halt. He felt quite at ease to be leaving home and, using the railway warrant sent to him by the army, caught the train from here to Oxford. Expecting to find transport arranged from Oxford station to Cowley Barracks, Frank was surprised to find the station almost deserted. On talking to a porter he found there was no vehicle to meet this particular train and realised that he would have to walk. The man pointed up the road that led out of the station and told him that if he kept walking that way he would eventually get to Cowley.

At that time Frank was not at all familiar with Oxford. He walked up to Carfax and checked his directions with a passer-by; he walked on down the High Street and asked again at the junction beyond the bridge; he walked on up the Cowley Road and at St. John's church was at last told, after walking for an hour and a half, that if he went up Hollow Way he would see the Barracks in front of him. At the gate he was questioned by a Lance-Corporal and directed to a room where he signed up to join Number One Company of the Ox and Bucks regiment. Standing alongside was the next new recruit, by coincidence also called Hall. This young soldier was given the next number to Frank, who was 5392920, so the two became known as Hall 20 and Hall 21. Although Hall 21 was actually called Peter, first names were rarely used in the army. Names like 'Smudger' Smith and 'Chalkie' White were the norm.

Number One Company was housed in thirteen huts alongside the football field. Frank and his companions were put into the thirteenth hut, next to a little lane running through to a pub on Horspath Road.

On the following morning, a Saturday, the new recruits were told to line up on the parade ground so that inoculations and battledress could be organised. The men were taken to the quartermaster's stores where they were sized up by eye and given a uniform to try on. Frank took his new outfit down to the barrack room and discovered that his trousers were about a foot too long. Back he went to the store to see the quartermaster who told him he would have to have another pair and said, "Take 'em off then."

Looking around at the ATS girls who worked in the store Frank asked, "Where?"

To which he got the sharp reply: "Take 'em off just there – they've seen it all before."

The young man, feeling he'd had his life broadened after just one day in the army, stripped off and stepped into his new trousers.

The uniforms gave off a dreadful smell of disinfectant. For the first five or six days it hung around the new recruits, making it easy to tell who had just joined up. Whether in the barracks or in the centre of Oxford the young soldiers could be sniffed out and identified as still wet behind the ears.

On Sunday morning Frank went out with the others to line up for the first drill. His eighteen months' training with the Home Guard soon caught the attention of the sergeant who asked him when he had joined up.

"Two days ago, with all the others," answered Frank and explained about his experience gained with the LDV, and his sergeant who fought with the Ox and Bucks in the 1914-18 war. Already familiar with the drills, marches and all the parts of a rifle and a grenade, Frank felt he had a head start over some of the other men.

He soon settled into Hut 13 and slept soundly in his hard bed with its three 'biscuits' (square-shaped solid cushions pushed together to make a mattress), a pillow stuffed with straw, a blanket to lie on and two over the top. The first pay-day came around and Frank opened his envelope to find twelve shillings. Since he was expecting fourteen this was a bit disappointing and he questioned the amount. He was told that two shillings had been deducted for the railway warrant as it had been issued by mistake. Apparently Stonesfield was too near to Oxford to qualify for subsidised travel. This explained why no-one met Frank at Oxford station on his first day.

Reveille was sounded at six every morning and the regime was strict, with plenty of shoe-shining and button-polishing. But because of his experience and willingness to learn Frank was made up to Lance-Corporal. He enjoyed this and soon found it to his advantage. When the soldiers went for their weekly ten-mile walk, Lance-Corporal Hall had no pack to carry on his back nor even a rifle to hold – he simply walked alongside the rest of the men, making sure they all kept up the pace. Training often took place on Shotover hill where the company learned how to set the sights on their rifles, checking the all-important distances: foreground, middle distance and background.

The importance of these three points had to be remembered at all times, along with three other vital things. These were a soldier's number and the rather odd phrase: 'HP sauce in Big Brown Bottles.' The capital letters served as a memory aid.

'H': Have a good field of fire.
'P': Permit free use of weapons.
'B': Be bullet-proof.
'B': Be inconspicuous.
'B': Be easy to advance from.

Then followed a jaunty little verse to be committed to memory:

'Knife, fork, spoon,
Razor, comb and lather brush,

Toothbrush, button stick and
Spare pair o' laces.'

Many ex-soldiers find it easier even now to remember these phrases, learned so long ago, than to forget.

Frank spent thirteen weeks at the Barracks, during which time he went home a couple of times. At the end of the first week a letter arrived from Aunt Edie telling him that Uncle George had pneumonia and was unable to work. George usually delivered meat to the surrounding villages for Mrs Tidmarsh and Alf Osborne had stepped in for him during Frank's first week away. However, Alf was unable to continue to help out so could Frank please come home? As soon as the letter arrived he took it to Sergeant-Major Williams who managed to get him a 36-hour pass. So at the weekend Frank was back in Stonesfield making sure that the meat got to the right customers.

By now Emma was also in uniform. She had joined the ATS and was stationed at Bardwell Road in Oxford with Southern Command HQ. By a remarkable coincidence the girl who joined immediately after her was also called Hall and her first name was Frances. Emma would catch the bus up to Cowley Barracks to see her brother and visit Frances' home which was in a street nearby.

8

At the end of week thirteen the soldiers were sent to the nearby Slade camp which was home to the Hampshire regiment. There were a few spare huts here and they housed the new recruits to the Ox and Bucks while they waited to join their 4th Battalion at Woodhall Spa in Lincolnshire. When the 4th Battalion returned from Dunkirk in 1940 they were severely depleted with only eighty men escaping death, capture or injury. They joined with the Gloucesters at Woodhall Spa and became a 'holding' battalion. During the war the Ox and Bucks had seven battalions and the Bucks another two. When soldiers like Frank had completed their initial instruction they went to the 4th for further extensive training before being sent to their final unit. They had to start from scratch so Frank lost his stripe now and went back to being

Private Hall although his spell as Lance-Corporal meant that he had a recommendation for promotion on his record.

The training turned out to be very hard indeed. When the men arrived at Woodhall Spa Halt they got off the train and thought that the waiting lorries were to take them the two and a half miles to the camp. But no, they were told to put their kitbags onto the lorries and line up. The soldiers marched to the camp and faced their new Sergeant-Major. His first words were those well-known to many young recruits: "I've never seen such a rabble in all my life!" Before they were allowed into camp he gave them half an hour's solid drilling in the road outside.

Once inside they could see the Nissen huts where they would live for the next three months. Made of tin, the huts were very prone to condensation and water ran down the inside of the curved walls. The Sergeant-Major allocated the men to their companies. Pointing to Frank, he said, "You - B Company."

After sorting this out, he then indicated a tin shed in a corner of the camp.

"By the way – your bedding. You'll find two palliases, one big, one small. That shed's full of straw. Use it to fill them up and how you sleep depends on how you do it. Cooked meal at 6 o'clock in the cookhouse and when you come out look on the company notice board to see what you're doing. Dismiss!"

The new members of B Company picked up their small packs and walked over to the shed to make their mattresses. When they found their Nissen hut they saw that the beds consisted of an iron frame and two wooden planks. Each man had been given three blankets and after making the beds with these the soldiers went for their meal.

Afterwards, when they looked at the notice board they discovered that B Company were part of a scheme and would be leaving at 12 o'clock that night. The following morning they were to 'attack' the aerodrome at Connersby. Frank took off his battledress, put on his lighter denim outfit and the company left at midnight to march the ten or twelve miles to their target.

At six the following morning the soldiers were smartening up and shaving in the river near Connersby. By seven they were 'attacking' the aerodrome, running towards the wire and sometimes being run over themselves. This was the first of many exercises. The soldiers stayed dressed in denim because they spent all their time outside. After a twenty-mile walk the following week the company went up to Sherwood Forest where they spent the week chasing Churchill tanks. They would dig a trench, lie in it and wait for a tank to pass overhead, chase after it to 'attack' and halt the tank whilst another trench was being dug in its path.

The commanding officer of B Company was Major Temple, an Oxfordshire man from Wendlebury. He noted that Frank had been a Lance-Corporal and offered him back his stripe. Frank said he would rather be a Private. At Woodhall Spa he had soon realised that if something went wrong the Sergeant blamed it on the Corporal who then blamed it on the Lance-Corporal. There were no privileges attached to the post of Lance-Corporal and the duties were about the same as a Private's, so a Private he would be.

Following the Sherwood Forest exercise, B Company marched 122 miles to Filingdales in Yorkshire. It took the soldiers five days to reach Filingdales where they spent a week 'field firing' using live ammunition. The rain that week was relentless and the men were not allowed to take shelter in the nearby huts. They were constantly wet and cold. At night each pair of soldiers would make a bivouac out of their two ground sheets and lie under it. One night Frank felt the water running underneath him as he lay trying to sleep. After four or five days at least fifteen of the men had pneumonia and the officer in charge decided that the company could spend the last two days sleeping in the huts.

Field firing meant running up a range for about 500 yards and firing live rounds from a Tommy gun. Each round deposited a brass cartridge on the ground and so two men had to run behind, picking them up. After Frank had practised firing twice, he took his turn at collecting cartridges. On his return the Corporal told him to go and do it again. Frank looked surprised and said to the Corporal, "I've just been once."

Unfortunately an officer was listening to this and he said straight away, "Put him on a charge!"

Because Frank had chosen to remain a Private, one of the other young soldiers had been made up to Lance-Corporal. The man came up to Frank in the evening and said,

"Hey Frank, I've got to put you on a charge but I don't know how to fill the Charge Sheet in!"

"Oh, that's all right", said Frank, "I'll show you." And filled in his own sheet.

The soldiers travelled back to camp by train. Frank had to stand in front of Major Temple and explain himself.

"I understand you were chattering and refused to do what the Corporal asked?" began the Major.

"No, I didn't refuse to go," Frank replied. "When the Corporal asked me to go, I only said that I'd just been already."

"Right," said Major Temple, "seven days' jankers."

So although there was nowhere to go, Private Hall nevertheless found himself confined to camp for a week. Fortunately, the first time Frank went to report to the guardroom he discovered that the Sergeant lived near Stonesfield at Long Hanborough and the two chatted a minute.

"Oh well," said the Sergeant, "you're not going to run away are you? Just report each morning and evening at 6 o'clock."

This was not too bad but Frank was still given extra duties. Instead of relaxing on an evening off he would spend his time peeling half a hundredweight of potatoes or collecting stones from the football field.

It was a hard life – the worst three months' of Frank's soldiering – and the young soldier wrote to his aunt: 'The Germans will never kill me because these up here will kill me first.'

Then B Company was asked for forty volunteers. The first twenty were needed for a battalion going to North Africa and the next to the 52nd, which was the 2nd battalion of Airborne Forces at Bulford in Wiltshire. Frank and his mate, Peter Hall, decided they wanted to get out as soon as possible and would volunteer for the first twenty. Hall 21 was accepted and was later to die out in Africa, but Frank was not. He said to Peter,

"Well, I'm not going to volunteer for the 2nd battalion because they fly about in gliders and I don't want that." Neither did anyone else. No-one volunteered.

A few days later Frank's name appeared with others on the notice board. All the men listed were told to report to the medical officer. Frank was examined and the officer wrote on his form 'A1+'. He asked the officer what it meant and was told that he was one of the fittest and therefore would be joining the Airborne battalion.

The twenty men chosen had to go by train to London. They picked up rations from the cookhouse and caught the train to King's Cross. There were two boxes of food, one containing cabbage and potatoes and the other one, which was given to Frank to carry, held a leg of lamb and a square of cake. At King's Cross the soldiers used the escalator and for some like Frank it was a new experience. Loaded with kitbags and rifles, they put the boxes down on the moving staircase. As the men reached the top they looked down and saw the bottoms of the boxes being ripped off and chewed up by the escalator mechanism. Cabbages and potatoes were rolling on the ground and back down the stairs. The decision was taken to abandon these but Frank managed to hang on to the cake and leg of lamb.

The soldiers went across to Waterloo station to catch a train to Salisbury. As they waited for the train an old lady stood on the platform eyeing the leg of lamb. Eventually she said, "That looks a nice piece of meat!"

Frank looked at her and said, "Well, you take it then."

Which only left the cake. By the time the train arrived the men were all so hungry that once on the move they decided to cut the cake and eat it. They were picked up at Salisbury and taken to Bulford where the Sergeant in charge asked where the rations were.

"We lost them at Waterloo station," replied the soldiers. The Sergeant accepted the explanation.

The new arrivals were sent to Wing barracks which was on a corner by the café. Next door was Marlborough, home of the Airborne Artillery, and opposite, next to the Picture Palace, was Kiwi which housed the Royal Ulster Rifles. And round about, all the different sections that made up a brigade, the main barracks being across the road. Until now there had been only one Airborne division, the First, made up of light infantry (who marched at 140 paces a minute) and heavy infantry (who marched at 120). However, as this division had gone to North Africa it was decided by the authorities to have another and this was called the Sixth Airborne, formed in the summer of 1942. Light and heavy infantry were separated and the Sixth was made up of light infantry from the Ox and Bucks, Royal Ulster Rifles and the Devons and they would be transported in gliders. Frank was in the MT (Motor Transport) section and was to serve with the Sixth until they were disbanded out in Palestine, where only thirteen remained, in 1946.

9

The Airborne divisions came from rather hesitant beginnings in 1940. The Prime Minister was very keen to develop an airborne force because the Germans had had divisions since 1936 and used them successfully to create confusion among the enemy ranks. So in 1940 parachutists began training and an order was placed with the aircraft industry for 400 Hotspur gliders.

Because the industry was so busy producing planes, the larger Horsa's would not be available until 1942. They had a circular fuselage made from a skin of plywood which was attached to numerous circular ribs of stouter wood. This wooden construction gave the gliders good buoyancy in water and some floated for quite a few hours if they came down in the sea. The Horsa could carry either twenty-eight men, who sat on wooden seats and carried no parachute, or a jeep and two trailers.

The first time Frank flew in a glider was in November 1942. Aeroplanes and gliders took off from nearby Netheravon. Waiting on the grass, because there was no tarmac here, were the small seven-seater Hotspurs used for training and the Halifax planes that pulled them into the air. The soldiers from Wing Barracks arrived one morning and were split into groups of seven. They watched as the Hotspurs took off at intervals, attached to the planes by a long tow-rope along which also ran a telephone wire. The men awaited the Sergeant's instructions to be ready to board as soon as the previous group returned.

As Frank and his six companions looked into the distance the Sergeant indicated a glider coming closer.

"That's yours," he said, "that's the one you'll be in when it comes down."

The plane circled and the glider pilot released the tow-rope. The Halifax flew off and the little Hotspur half-turned. But something went horribly wrong. The glider began to spin, spiralling straight down to the ground. Six men were killed instantly; the seventh died the following day.

Hard as it was, the training was not abandoned. Frank's group were told to board the next glider when it arrived about twenty minutes later. As they did so, about 200 yards away wreckage and bodies were being cleared from the area. The soldiers were quickly learning that in the army this kind of thing was all in a day's work.

Frank was not favourably impressed with his first flight. The glider was so small and light that he could feel every bump as the little wheels bounced along over the grass. Then suddenly all was quiet apart from the whistling of the wind and the Hotspur was high in the sky. The glider had to climb higher than the plane or it could get caught in the slipstream, oscillate violently and the rope could snap. So the soldiers looked down on the Halifax and the green fields as the light wooden glider swayed and bobbed in turbulence and air-pockets. Despite this Frank never felt sick in the air or on the sea. Sitting with twenty-seven others in the Horsa as they flew here and there, he would watch as first one and then another started to turn green and reach for the bag. Sometimes the stench was terrible and he tried to ignore it as best he could.

Bulford was a large camp with its headquarters in the nearby village and it lay within that area of Wiltshire where army and airforce activity was highly concentrated. The MT section usually flew out of Netheravon but there were other aerodromes all around at Way Hill, Middle Wallop and Thruxton where Dakotas flew out with paratroopers and panniers of ammunition. Up on Boscombe Down new aeroplanes were tested and put through their paces.

Frank and his companions in the billet were to stay together in Wing barracks for the best part of two years so they got to know each other very well. Just inside the door was Bill Reynolds, a Full Corporal who later met his death during the Normandy landings. Next to him was 'Woody' from Sevenoaks in Kent and two from London, Roy Frear and Johnny King. Johnny worked for Reuter's. Next came someone from closer to home – Ned Carr, who worked at MacFisheries in Headington, Oxford. A soldier with the rather grand name of John Charles Hugh Corbett was one of the last to join and had come from

Dunkirk. Travelling on round the room we come to two more Oxfordshire men, Johnny Walker and Bill Clelford, who used to cycle to Oxford from Bulford on a tandem when they had a weekend off.

Someone with a very unusual occupation was Waller and he was a 'Wall of Death' rider. The other men used to ask him about his job and he would tell them that it was the 'easiest thing in the world' to stay up there on that motorbike. The tremendous speed just kept him up there. At the top of the room was Jack Landon who lived at Headington and next to him, in the corner, was Jack Belton from Leicester. Next came two London barrow-boys, George Mash and 'Piggy' Bacon, who were of course known as Bacon 'n Mash. In the opposite corner was Vic Dowley from Fulbrook in Oxfordshire and then came three Remy chaps: Lance-Corporal Mann, Robbins, and Hunt who was married – he too was killed during the Normandy landings.

The last person to mention is Les Mitchell. He came from Cumnor Hill in Oxford and was employed by the City Council as a signwriter. Les put this skill to good use whilst he was in the Sixth Airborne. The regiment had as their emblem the flying horse, Pegasus, on the front and back of all its vehicles. If a horse needed replacing and there were no transfers available, then Les would paint it on by hand and the men were amazed at the accuracy of his work. Quite a few of the soldiers, including Les, had been called up in 1939 or '40 and so were considerably older than Frank. Every morning there was a three-mile run across Salisbury Plain and Les found this hard, being nearer thirty years old than twenty and rather tubby too. On a wet morning Frank and the other 'youngsters' would enjoy finding a nice deep puddle and splashing Les as he came panting along.

"You young b.....s!" he'd gasp, "You won't want to get up and run when you get to my age!"

If George Mash could get out of the 6.30am run he would. He would approach Corporal Bill Reynolds and offer to be 'Room Orderly'. This meant that he had to stay behind and tidy any unmade beds, sweep the floor ready for polishing and clean out the stove. The rest of the men would go off for their run but when they returned Mash had gone back to bed and was fast asleep with the room just as they had left it. People started talking about this and their grumbles reached the sharp ears of Company Sergeant-Major Wally Bourne, a man small in stature but a feared and respected regular soldier. One morning he looked along the line of soldiers from the MT section and said, "Where's Mash?"

"He's Room Orderly, Sir," came the reply.

The CSM marched smartly across to the barrack block, flung open the door – but found the room empty. George had been looking out of the window to see when the men went off for their run so that he could nip back into bed. When he saw Company Sergeant-Major Bourne striding towards the door he panicked. In the middle of the floor stood a broom cupboard with two doors and quick as a flash, wearing only a shirt, he ran in, closed the doors and held his breath.

But the CSM was as crafty as the private and threw open the cupboard doors to reveal the missing soldier.

"What are you doing in there Mash?" barked Wally.

"Scrounging, Sir," replied George.

Company Sergeant-Major Bourne told him it was a good thing he had told the truth – otherwise he would have marched him over to the Orderly room where the military police had cells for soldiers who would not toe the line. A man would be kept under lock and key until he came up before his commanding officer. George had escaped this fate by being honest but after the event Corporal Reynolds said to him, "That's it Mashy! You're never being Room Orderly again because you d… well don't do it and you got me into trouble. So tomorrow morning you'll be out!" He was.

The soldiers always wore plimsolls for the morning run but one morning, as the men lined up, Sergeant-Major Bourne noticed that one of them was wearing his boots. When questioned, the young man replied that he was waiting for a new pair of plimsolls.

"Oh go back in," said the CSM. "You can't run with your boots on."

Frank heard this and began to think that he would rather like a morning off, too.

Bright and early the following day he laced up his boots and went to line up with the others. Wally looked down at Private Hall's feet.

"Hall," he said, "why have you got your boots on?"

"Oh, my plimsolls are in for replacement," Frank replied.

Once again the Sergeant-Major proved too difficult to out-manoeuvre and he said to Frank, "That won't hurt for once. You'll be all right in them this morning."

So it was a hard run that morning but Les Mitchell found Frank's discomfort very amusing and had a good laugh now the boot was on the other foot, so to speak.

But it was all good fun and no matter what difficult times were to follow the soldiers never forgot the camaraderie they shared together.

Occasionally they would part company and go back home on leave. Apart from Walker and Clelford who rode home on the tandem, most of the chaps used the train.

The 9.22 pm train from Waterloo became known as the Airborne Special. Frank would take a train to Reading, hoping to catch an earlier connection, but nine times out of ten he saw the back of it disappearing out of the station as he arrived. This meant a wait of nearly two hours for the 9.22. The train went to Plymouth and on the way dropped off its last two carriages at Basingstoke where they were attached to a smaller engine and pulled down the branch line to Bulford. Frank had left home at four in the afternoon and catching the Airborne Special meant that he arrived back in camp at 1.30 or 2 o'clock in the morning instead of 9.00pm as he always hoped. Getting off the train at Bulford Sidings, the men would take the short cut and on a moonlit night he could look across the fields and see up to one hundred and fifty shadowy figures making their weary way back to camp.

Soon however, all thoughts of leave were forgotten as the time of the D-Day landings approached and this was to be Frank's first experience of combat overseas.

10

In the summer of 1943 the Sixth were sent down to Ilfracombe for six weeks' extensive training. This involved a twenty-two mile march every week and exercises like firing out to sea. The soldiers were also used in the making of a film for the War Office. They would be dropped out in the sea, wade ashore between Ilfracombe and Combe Martin and climb up the rocks using ropes, all for the benefit of the cameras. At the end of five weeks the companies began the march back to Bulford but Frank, being in the MT section, was spared this

The MT section at Ilfracombe (Frank is first on the left in the middle row)

and drove back.

When autumn came the Airborne divisions were at last ready to be trained for the opening of the war's final stage – the invasion of Europe. By spring 1944 they felt confident and well-prepared to begin this mighty task. The crossings over the River Orne and the Caen Canal needed to be taken and training for this difficult operation had taken place in Oxfordshire because the area around Aston and Bampton was very much like the Normandy countryside where the two bridges were situated. The main problem concerning the Airborne commanders was always the weather. Meteorological experts had given their opinion that, bearing in mind also the state of the tides, the 5th and 6th of June would be suitable dates.

So in the middle of a warm June night the soldiers from Wing barracks assembled in the darkness on the parade ground. As always, they went off without knowing where they were headed or whether it was to be actual combat or another exercise. Frank had been sent down to Winterbourne Gunner so that all the MT section's vehicles could be waterproofed. The exhaust pipes were turned so that they finished up near the windscreen and all the working parts were covered with a kind of plasticine substance. If the troops landed in water they would need to know that they could drive out onto dry land successfully, but then the proofing had to be removed as quickly as possible or the engine would overheat.

Once on the road, the soldiers realised that they were driving towards London. When they arrived in the city a police escort was waiting. Traffic on all the major roads was halted whilst the army vehicles sped through. The convoy came to rest and the men waited for dawn. At first light they realised that they were in a large parkland area. The soldiers washed, shaved and breakfasted, speculating amongst themselves about the purpose of the journey. No-one was allowed to venture from the camp and no-one, neither the Corporal nor anyone they asked, knew anything. Eventually darkness fell.

Once again the company fell in and were told to get into the vehicles. They drove for three or four hours before entering an area of grassland. Something about the surroundings felt familiar and Frank said to his mate, "Do you know, I'm sure we're back in the same place we were in last night!"

Frank's mate felt the same and they decided they must have travelled in a big circle and come back to where they had started. No-one could understand this and the men spent another day in the park waiting for nightfall. When it was dark they set off again, this time to arrive at Tilbury docks where a boat and cranes were waiting.

Jeeps and trailers were loaded into the ship's hold where they were strapped down securely. The soldiers boarded the ship and bedded down for the night in canvas boats which stood on the deck. As always when the Airborne forces needed to go abroad, half of the men would fly and the other half would travel by sea. Travelling in the gliders was dangerous and it was expected that some would be lost. So as an insurance the soldiers were split into two groups and these groups alternated between sea and air. Frank was glad he was in the sea-borne section this time. He took turns with Vic Dowley, from Fulbrook, and it had been Vic's turn to fly.

The commanders had wanted to begin on June 4th but the weather forecast was not good so things were delayed by a day. When the soldiers heard about the plans some time later they guessed that this was the reason for the extra day spent in the park. Late in the night of June 5th six Halifax planes and gliders took off from England and those gliders landed quietly in France. The first glider to land early on June 6th carried Major Howard of D Company and touched down close to the canal bridge, afterwards known as the Pegasus bridge. The Paras, along with the Light Infantry and Royal Engineers, seized the crossings on the Orne and the Caen Canal, along with the surrounding area. Both bridges were taken quickly but the men were finding it increasingly difficult to hold on to them. They were very relieved when they saw the main army coming out of the sea.

It was Day Three when Frank and his comrades arrived in France. The boat had a large, level area made of metal sheets, bolted together. The army vehicles were hoisted onto this platform and the boat sailed as close as it could to the land. When it could edge no closer the front was lowered and the soldiers drove their jeeps through the water and up the sandbank. Up on the beach an officer hurried them along, calling,

"Right – follow in, follow in, follow in...."

The last driver of the Ox and Bucks was Frank. Behind him came the first vehicle of the Royal Ulster Rifles. Suddenly there was an explosion on the track and Frank looked round to find that this jeep and trailer had gone, having hit a landmine. The officer called out, "Carry on – carry on!"

So the convoy drove on and soon joined up with the advance party at Ampreville. The weary Paras had had a hard time and were very pleased to see that help had arrived.

The new arrivals joined up with the rest of the MT Section which had been flown in and drove on to Breville Wood. Here, the battalion held the high ground with the Paras and Lord Lovatt Commandos for eleven to twelve weeks. This enabled the sea-borne forces to enter the area. A, B, C and D company were stationed on the perimeter with Frank's MT section behind. The soldiers felt again that they were being told nothing and just carried on with their tasks, unaware of what the men on the boundary were doing. A jeep would be called for to take Captain so-and-so to C company or perhaps an officer wanted to be taken to Brigade HQ but other than that the men stuck to their duties. For six weeks they had no bread but instead lived on their 'compo' rations: a tin containing cigarettes, chocolate, bully beef, dry biscuits and tinned treacle pudding.

The empty tins proved useful. A wire was stretched between the trees, about eighteen inches above ground level, and on here the men hung their tins. Each pair of soldiers dug a small trench nearby and this is where they spent the nights. In the stillness a metallic sound would have them quickly alert and ready to deal with any intruders. Although the trenches were close together the men were advised not to talk because sounds carried easily so the long night usually passed in silence. Sleep began to be a thing of the past. The men would 'Stand To' night and morning but between the hours of six in the evening and six in the morning each man watched for an hour on, then an hour off. No sooner had Frank fallen asleep than he felt himself being shaken awake again for his turn on watch.

One night the men were alerted by firing and wondered what was happening. A large troop of soldiers was coming down the road towards them. Captain Busher rushed out saying, "Get out there and stop them!"

When the men asked why he answered, "We're being attacked – there are thousands of Germans up there!"

Apparently Major Edmonds from B company, thinking there were only a few Germans holding the next ridge, had decided to attack and take it. (The men only found out about this later.) As B company came up out of the dip the Germans opened fire. There were many more enemy troops than expected and that night two or three officers died along with a Sergeant-Major Crew. Major Edmonds was one of those injured, his neck scorched by a grenade explosion, but the injuries and deaths had been to no avail – nothing had been gained.

But more often the long dark hours were quiet, the air filled with tension. After a night of catnaps it was time for a full day's work. When the battalion had been in the wood for fourteen days Captain Busher came to Frank and his mate, Lance Corporal Vic Dowley, and said, "I've got a job for you – and it's not very nice."

When the pair asked what kind of work it was he said, "We've got to bury the dead."

So Frank and Vic began the harrowing job of seeking out the bodies and bringing them back for burial.

The Company Commanders knew where soldiers had been killed and with this information the two young men would go out with a jeep and three stretchers to fetch them. Two were laid in the back and one across the bonnet, the operation being repeated many times. In Breville Wood there was a large, flat-bottomed hole left behind by the Germans who had dug it out to house a gun. It was into this mortar pit that the bodies were brought and placed heads to feet. Altogether, Frank and Vic recovered ninety-eight dead German soldiers' bodies. Every time a body was brought in the Padre would be there to perform a proper burial service.

Many bodies were badly injured and incomplete and the two men composed them as best they could. Identification could have been difficult were it not for a metal disc that each wore round his neck. The disc could be broken in half across a line of perforations. One of these halves had to be tied to the body; the other to a small sandbag into which Frank and Vic would put the soldier's personal belongings. The bag was given to the Company Commander who passed it to Brigade, Division and so on until the enemy were finally informed of the soldier's death. Before Frank buried the first body he took out the man's wallet and opened it. Inside was a photograph of a woman with two little girls, his wife and daughters. He stood there, thoughts of the dreadful waste of life washing over him. He did not want to be there; the German soldier had not wanted to be there – it just had to be done. Frank decided not to look at personal items any more.

As well as burying the enemy soldiers the young Private and Lance Corporal had to bury the bodies of the fallen British and they did this awful job daily for three weeks. One of their own, Bill Parsons, was killed in the wood. He was going out with a jeep and trailer piled with landmines when a shell struck the vehicle and caused a huge explosion. Bill was just twenty-two and came from Charlbury. Major Howard, the first officer to land in France on June 5th to take the bridges, was their Company Commander and said to Frank and Vic, "I wouldn't have a job like you've got. Is there anything we can do for you?"

It would have been nice to have a bit of a break from the work but Frank just said it would be good to have some more cigarettes. The weather was hot and the stench was terrible. Often the German bodies would be lying in 'no man's land' so the two young men had to wait until dusk to recover them. Then they would come across decomposing cows and horses that had been killed and the air was thick with mosquitoes, rising like smoke into the air. The two soldiers worked at their gruesome task each day while the company was stationed in Breville Wood.

From the wood they moved on to the orchard of a farm that had been taken. Company HQ was in the farmyard opposite. Their route ran across 'Bomb Alley crossroads' – a crossing that the Germans would shell all day every day at regular intervals, knowing that the British had to use it frequently. The British army retaliated by doing the same.

Captain Busher offered Frank an Italian lorry that had belonged to the Germans, to replace his jeep and trailer. Not only was there far more room on the lorry for ammunition, rations and petrol, it was also used to take men from the different companies down to the sea for a break.

The orchard was set on high ground and in the low ground below there was an artillery battery armed with four inch mortars. One night the MT section heard the sound of mortars for about fifteen minutes. No-one knew why but later the men were told that the mortars were being fired across no-man's-land in an attempt to dislodge the Germans from their forward position. The enemy started firing back shells and the explosive noise continued for two and a half or three hours. Frank crouched in his trench thinking that this would be the end of the war and probably of himself. About halfway through the onslaught Frank heard someone shuffling towards the trench. It was Captain Busher on all fours, checking his men.

"Who's in there?"

"Hall and Varney, sir."

"Are you all right?"

"Yes sir."

"We've lost Corporal Reynolds. He's just been killed."

Bill Reynolds had been about fifty yards from Frank in a trench near a tree. A shell had hit the tree and the blast was directed back towards the Corporal's trench. Bill had lived with his wife and daughter near Lechlade at Buscot and his wife was soon to give birth to their next child. He was killed on June 25th.

However, Frank and many of the others survived and stayed where they were until it was time to move on and make the journey from the River Orne to the Seine.

11

The Third Armoured Division came in and made use of the gliders for cover before they made an advance through the Falaise gap and on to Paris. On reaching Paris the English and Canadians dropped down the far side of the River Seine and the troops on the high ground began to advance, trapping one hundred and twenty thousand German soldiers on the marshy ground between the two rivers. The operation took four days and prisoners were taken by the hundred.

Frank was driving the big Italian lorry loaded with petrol, rations and ammunition that he collected from Brigade HQ. He had to pick up a Quartermaster Sergeant from the Company Commanders' headquarters and wait for night to fall. Then the Sergeant would accompany Frank, directing him to all the different companies where they dropped off rations. Two people were needed to start the lorry's engine – one to wind the handle in front and one to pull the lever inside the cab. This meant that when deliveries were made Frank had to leave the engine running. The first time he did this the officer from the company rushed out saying, "Shut that b..... thing off!"

Frank explained that he would not be able to restart it so then the officer told him, "Well hurry up and get off then!"

So Frank unloaded first the ammunition, then the petrol followed by the food and got back into the lorry as quickly as he could. The Quartermaster's company was always the last port of call and he left the lorry at this point, thanking Frank and telling him to get back now to Brigade HQ. As much as thirty miles could have been covered as the troops advanced during the day but HQ was still in the same place, making the round trip very lengthy. Not only did Frank have to drive at least sixty miles in total; he also had to do this in darkness and without the use of headlamps. Although it was strange at first his eyes soon became accustomed to relying on the meagre light from the moon and stars. But because progress in the dark was slow and the distances were so long Frank hardly slept at all for four days.

On the second evening his companion was the Quartermaster from A company. This man was new in post, his predecessor having been lost in battle. He was unsure of his bearings and some way into the journey the lorry was stopped by a patrol. Out of the darkness came the question:

"What are you doing up here? This is No-Man's Land!"

Frank explained that they were trying to find A Company.

"Well they're half a mile back that way," said the soldier. "You've crossed over our lines."

Somehow Private Hall drove the lorry back along the dark tracks, its engine sounding very loud in the still night. But the journey was uneventful and Frank felt fortunate to arrive back safely.

He had another lucky escape on the third night. While he was out of the lorry delivering the rations he was suddenly startled by a loud bang. A mortar bomb had fallen in front of the vehicle, tearing two pieces out of the radiator and all the glass from the windscreen. The Quartermaster told him he ought to get back to base so Frank drove off alone, water gradually leaking from the lorry. Arriving at a crossroads he was unsure which direction to take. Something seemed to tell him to turn right so he put the engine into second gear and travelled slowly down this road for about two and a half hours. In the early hours of the morning he came across Vic Dowley. Vic, as well as being a Lance-Corporal, was also a dispatch rider and had been out on his motorbike looking for Frank. Amazingly, Frank had been driving in the right direction and – once again – felt very lucky. His radiator was patched up, ready for the fourth night's work and on this night the troops reached the Seine.

Jimmy James, the Lieutenant-Quartermaster, had been killed in Breville Wood. The Regimental Quartermaster, Bill Aldsworth, took on his job and knew that Frank had been working very hard to keep people supplied. To show his appreciation he told him to bring his mug round for a drink. So Frank picked up his enamel mug and strolled round to see the officer. Lieutenant-Quartermaster Aldsworth filled half the mug with rum, saying, "Drink that – it'll do you the world of good."

At twenty-one, Private Hall had never drunk spirits in his life but he drained the mug obediently, said his thanks and retired to bed. At 2 o'clock in the morning he woke up feeling ill. In fact he felt so bad he wished a German would come round the corner and shoot him. It was the first and last time he ever touched spirits.

The Lieutenant-Quartermaster had also told Frank that the job here was finished and they would all be going back to Blighty on the following Monday – and this was definite, not a rumour. If the men wanted any clothes they ought to take them now. So they took off the battledress they had worn for so long and changed into clean suits and clean underwear. These soldiers were the first to be issued with string vests. They were supposed to let the skin breathe through the large holes but at the same time trap warmth. The chance of clean clothes was a great relief to Frank whose own were tainted with the stains and smells of all the dead he had carried and buried. The only thing he had been able to wash had been his shirt. Up in the wood, he had remarked on his stinking shirt to Varney and the two came up with the idea of washing their shirts in the nearby stream. They took them off, rinsed them in the water and then, one at each end of the wet clothes, wrung and pulled until they could get no more water out. In the warmth of the summer they felt great as they pulled on their damp shirts, saying, "That's better!"

They returned to England as promised on September 3rd, a memorable day for Frank as it was his Aunt Annie's birthday and the date the war had started. He would always have vivid memories of this first operation.

After a well-deserved leave of seven days Frank travelled back to Bulford to find quite a number of new faces replacing those killed or injured. The routine at camp continued as it had before. In the middle of December he wrote home to Aunt Edie to say he was lucky enough to have leave for Christmas and was looking forward to his dinner at home. Around December 21st the Battle of the Bulge was taking place in the Ardennes and the Americans were suffering. They requested help.

The Sixth Airborne had been back from Normandy for a few months now and had been rebuilt to full strength. The division was chosen to return to France. So instead of arriving home in Stonesfield, on Christmas Eve Frank found himself driving on to the shore at Calais at 10 o'clock in the morning. It was cold, there was no heating in the big lorries and it was a miserable journey. Dried food and compo rations had taken the place of a hot Christmas dinner. Passing through a large town that night the soldiers saw plenty of French people, dressed in their best black clothes and on their way to Midnight Mass. They were pleased to think that at least these folk were now liberated. The convoy met up with the Americans on Boxing Day.

The Sixth remained in the Ardennes for three months. During that time Frank never saw a blade of grass; all was ice and snow. In order to camouflage the tanks they were painted white. The soldiers were stationed at a place called Blerique where they stayed in a big granary. The cold was intense. If a driver had forgotten to put on his gloves in the morning his hand would stick to the door handle of the vehicle. The company was spread about into its usual sections of A, B, C and D and the conditions made it very difficult to move stores between them.

About twenty miles back in the direction they had travelled was a railway station. Here, the Americans kept some vehicles called 'Weasels', about the size of a jeep but with tracks that covered two-thirds of the base. They were steered with two sticks on the left side and could glide easily over soft mud or snow. Frank travelled down with the MT section to pick up some of these and soon appreciated the beauty of the vehicles. With the Weasel, delivering rations was much easier.

Although the soldiers were there to help the Americans they had very little contact with them, but during the three months casualties among the British were quite heavy. Hearing the usual rumours later on it seemed that when the men made a push toward a certain area they had sometimes been misinformed about the numbers of German soldiers they would find. When expecting just a few they were occasionally seriously outnumbered and lost men as a result. So the forward troops were grateful when they were given a break of forty-eight hours and the opportunity of a weekend in Brussels.

The MT Section drove them to the city. The army vehicles were secured in a compound during the day so the men were free to explore and spent their time sightseeing and relaxing in the cafés with a beer. The single men stuck together but Frank noticed that the married men found other places to visit where they found a different kind of enjoyment. None knew when they would see their wives again, or even if, so they just lived for the moment and took the comfort offered to them. For some the war would affect their marriages badly as not only husbands but wives at home were unfaithful, but for others it was just an interlude and they returned to a happy family life.

In March Frank came back to England and made his delayed visit home to Stonesfield. The next operation was Arnhem and although the Sixth Airborne stood by it was the First who were sent this time. The Sixth waited but were never called as the First eventually returned, stopped at the Nijmegen bridges. But the war was progressing rapidly now and the British were ready to cross the River Rhine. In May the Sixth were called to action and the MT section prepared their biggest vehicles for the journey. As they did so, the men put their own words to the song 'Bless 'em All' and soon everyone was singing it:

'They say there's a glider about to take off
Bound for old Germanee.
Heavily laden with Oxford and Bucks,
They go by glider because they can't go by truck.
So we're saying Goodbye to them all
As up the runway they crawl,
You'll get no propellors you unlucky fellas
So cheer up my lads – bless 'em all!'

12

This time it was Frank's turn to fly; Vic Dowley was due to go by sea. The force was not to be identified as the Airborne Division and so the Pegasus emblem was painted out on the vehicles and the men's distinctive red berets exchanged for khaki.

Lorries were laden with supplies and equipment and those going by sea were due to leave a fortnight before those flying so that there would be plenty of time to drive the vehicles to Germany. Just before this was due to happen, Frank and Vic were on a forty-eight hour pass. Frank got home on Friday evening and on Saturday morning a telegram arrived, recalling him to Bulford. He was told to report to the nearest railway station and when he arrived at Oxford the Military police were waiting to usher him onto the train.

At the same time a telegram arrived at Vic's house in Fulbrook. Vic, however, was not at home because he was courting a girl in Birmingham and had gone straight there. His mother was not too concerned as she was expecting him back on Sunday and thought she would give it to him then. When Frank got to Bulford Captain Busher told him that Vic Dowley had not returned and Frank must take his place on a scheme. He would be leaving by sea on Sunday. So for the second time, Frank was spared the flight. Meanwhile, back in Fulbrook, Vic was reading the telegram that had ordered him back to camp. He returned on the next train, wondering what Captain Busher would say, but the Captain told him not to worry; "Hall's taken your place, so you'll have to fly instead of him."

Two weeks later Vic flew off and was unlucky enough to end up with a piece of shrapnel in his backside. Somehow, he managed (good-humouredly) to pin the blame for this onto Frank, although Frank felt that Mrs Dowley should have shouldered more responsibility than himself.

With only a piece of shrapnel to worry about, Vic had been lucky. Waiting in his lorry to cross the Rhine, Frank watched as German incendiary bullets hit some of the gliders. The wooden structure caught fire and the soldiers, without parachutes, dropped to the ground. Those Paras who landed safely captured the bridgehead and built a pontoon bridge over the river. The lorries crossed the river immediately and met up with them. Although it was May, the weather was appalling. Heavy rain turned the ground to mud. As Frank drove along he met ambulances bringing the wounded back to the Red Cross tent. Here, soldiers were laid out in rows in the rain, waiting for help which sometimes came too late. The situation was bad. A company of Scottish Paras had got caught up in trees as they were landing and were shot as they hung there helpless.

Private Hall drove on, leaving the chaos behind him. Lieutenant-Quartermaster Aldsworth had asked Captain Busher if he could have Frank's help again. Later, sitting beside him in the lorry, Bill Aldsworth was reading the map as they headed in the direction of Munster, aiming towards a particular spot. As they drove into the town they passed one or two tanks and eventually arrived in the centre. On seeing the lorry, an officer popped out of one of the tanks and shouted: "What are you doing up here?"

The Lieutenant-Quartermaster told him they were trying to find a certain map reference.

"Well I think you're reading the b..... map wrong!"

When Bill questioned why he should think this the officer answered, "Because we've got a tank battle on with the Germans just here! Our tanks are up here, the German tanks are down there – so I think you're in the wrong b..... place!"

Without further ado they were told to get out of the b..... way, get back to where they came from and find out where they were supposed to be going.

Frank reversed the lorry but found he could not get down the road because of all the tanks coming up. Bill said, "We'd better wait here then, Hall."

To which Frank replied, "No, I'm not sitting in here with that lot about – if a shell comes over we're gone!"

He looked around and spotted a building that looked like a town hall.

"We'll go in there," he said.

When the two got inside they found the interior hung with long banners, decorated with the German swastika. Frank decided that this was an opportunity to take a souvenir and climbed up and released one of them. He rolled up the banner which was about fifteen feet long and kept it with him until he returned to Stonesfield, where it still resides today, having even been used for a while as a bedspread by Frank's son, Stephen.

When the battle was over the two men got back in the lorry and Lieutenant-Quartermaster Aldsworth found that the map reference pointed them to a farm. Turning left, they soon entered a farmyard and this was where the MT section was to muster and pick up all the rations and supplies. After about half an hour Captain Busher came in and said that he wanted three or four men to go up to the main road. The ground in the entrance to the farm had become rather soft. A lorry had turned into the gateway and had fallen sideways into a tree on the left-hand side. Now it was stuck and blocking the road.

The Captain had found an old wooden jack down at the farm and Frank accompanied him to the entrance.

The men used the jack to put wooden planks under the lorry in the hope that it could be driven away once level. This seemed to be working but as Frank pushed in the last plank the whole lot collapsed. He found himself pressed down into a ditch with the wood across his shoulder and a piece sticking into his back, driving him down into the mud. His shoulder was dislocated but the tree saved him from being completely crushed. He was in the ditch for about an hour and a half until a lorry with a winch arrived. A rope was tied round the tilted vehicle and it was pulled upright, enabling the men to lift the soldier out.

Captain Busher put Frank into a jeep and took him to a medical station. The young man was in great pain from his injuries but the Captain had to drive him back into Munster to the station there. When they arrived the Medical Officer gave Frank an injection 'to ease the pain' and the next thing he was aware of was waking up gradually to find himself in a room with other patients. Some of those in the adjoining beds were German because the Red Cross helped anyone who was injured, regardless of which side they were fighting for. His shoulder had been put back into place and after a short rest he was taken to a big house the Red Cross were using.

When he arrived his helpers were told to take him upstairs. Frank was unable to walk and so he had to be carried on a stretcher. Near the top of the staircase one of the bearers lost his footing and everyone, including the patient, slid back down to the bottom. A very large lady, possibly a doctor, looked down at Frank and asked him if he was all right. Frank, who had parted company with the stretcher, told her he was a little bit sore, so she looked at the bearers sternly and said, "Right, take him up again – and be b..... careful this time!"

At the second attempt the climb was successful and Frank was put into a bed on the first floor. Feeling thirsty he asked a ward orderly for a drink of water. The man went off to fetch one but never returned. However, in the Red Cross all differences are put aside and German medical staff worked alongside the British and other nationalities. Frank asked one of the Germans for his drink and this man brought it straight away.

The house stood close to an airfield. From here Dakotas, kitted out as ambulance planes, flew the wounded home to England. On the morning after his arrival a flight was due to leave and Frank heard someone call out the name 'Belton'. He wondered, could it be Jack Belton who had been with him only the day before? They had been in a convoy and were held up by hundreds of very young German soldiers who walked across their path. The young men kept asking, "Where have we got to go?"

None of the waiting soldiers knew the answer and so they told them to just keep walking. Jack Belton was standing patiently between two lorries when another lorry drove up and hit the one behind him, pushing it into him and crushing his ribs. Jack, like Frank, had been taken away for medical help. When a man was carried past his bed on a stretcher Frank called out, "Is that you Jack?"

Jack, surprised by the familiar voice, asked, "What are you doing here Frank?"

Frank told him that he had had a bit of an accident yesterday and Jack asked if he was coming back to Blighty.

"No, I don't think so," said Frank. Jack told him that he was just going back on the plane so they took leave of each other and Frank wished him good luck, saying he would see him sometime.

As it happened, he left that day too. He was put on to a hospital train bound for Ghent in Belgium. The Red Cross had taken over a big school here and Private Hall was given one of about a hundred beds in a very large room. The nurses in this makeshift hospital had plenty to do so they were very glad of any help the patients could give. Frank was able to walk about now and look after himself and after he had washed and shaved he joined with the other more able-bodied in helping the staff care for the sick.

There was an Ak-Ak battery in the vicinity of the school and there were quite a number of ATS girls here. Many of these girls gave up their free day every week to come and help at the hospital, making endless cups of tea and cheering those who had lost their limbs.

Frank was sent from here to convalesce near Dunkirk. Here, the Doctors concentrated on making injured bodies strong again and exercise and physiotherapy were used intensively. Frank's shoulder was strengthened by games of table tennis which he always enjoyed and very soon he was sent home on hospital leave.

13

When the time came for him to leave, Dunkirk was buzzing with rumours. The men had heard that the end of the war was at last in sight. Frank's comrades in Munster had gone to Berlin and met up with the Russians and it seemed that the Germans were finally beaten.

As Private Hall sailed across the Channel for his leave peace was declared. But the homecoming soldiers were unable to join in all the celebrations of VE night because the ship was ordered to drop anchor outside Tilbury dock until things had quietened down. The next morning the soldiers left the boat and were taken by train to Sunningdale, in Berkshire. Organisation here was very efficient and within two hours of arriving the men had been paid, fed and given passes to go home. It seemed that Frank was back in Stonesfield in no time at all and it was good to spend ten days in the comfort of home.

At the end of his leave he returned to Sunningdale and prepared to rejoin the regiment. An Airborne Sergeant caught site of his red beret and asked where he was going. When Frank told him he was going back to the Sixth Airborne the man said,

"Well – they're coming back on Monday."

"Are you sure?" asked Frank.

The Sergeant told him that it was definite and that if he were to leave now he would miss them. Frank wanted to be sure about things and so the man went away to check. After half an hour he said yes, the regiment would return on Monday and Frank was to take a train to Bulford.

When he arrived back in camp Sergeant-Major Bourne took one look at him and demanded to know: "What are you doing here, Hall? You're supposed to be over there!"

Frank explained and the Sergeant-Major told him that the MT section would not be arriving until the following Thursday. Perhaps he would like to go on leave? The soldier thought he had had enough leave for now and waited at Bulford for the vehicles' return. The rest of the regiment duly arrived on Monday and most went on leave. They were surprised to see Frank and keen to hear news of Jack Belton.

On Thursday Frank was reunited with his vehicle. The first thing he did was look under the driver's seat and there, safely stowed away, was his German banner. Another memento picked up along the way was a German officer's cap but this had been taken and was now someone else's souvenir.

Crossing the parade ground at night, Frank was stopped by the MT Officer who asked if he had read the Regimental Orders.

"No Sir," said Frank, "I never read Regimental Orders."

"Well, this time you'd better read them," said the Officer.

The Private found the orders and discovered that he would no longer have this rank. 5392920 Private Hall had been made up to a full Corporal.

Frank sought out Captain Busher's Batman, Jack, in his hut at the top of the square where all regimental badges and paraphernalia were sewn on. Corporal Hall asked if he would help him by sewing on his new stripes. The job was done straight away and the following morning Frank's mates raised their eyebrows as the new Corporal walked into the cookhouse.

Shortly after the end of the war in Europe the soldiers were sent home on leave. But it was decided that the First and Sixth Airborne would join together in an air operation on Japan, where fighting continued. So after only four or five days at home, Frank was recalled to camp. A big meeting was held in the gym where an officer told the men that they would be facing a different kind of war in Japan and British casualties could reach eighty per cent. Over the next few days the soldiers were kitted out with their tropical gear and heard that the advance party had already gone to Burma. But the Sixth never got to Japan. As they were preparing to leave, the Americans dropped their bomb on Hiroshima and the Japanese capitulated. The Airborne troops were spared the jungle fighting and the expected casualties.

However, preparations had been made and these would not be wasted. Towards the end of 1945 there was trouble in Palestine and it was decided that the Airborne soldiers could help out there instead. It took about ten days to sail to Haifa in Palestine. From here the men drove in open trucks to Gaza where they were to spend a few weeks before moving on to 120 Maintenance Unit in Nathania, and on to Camp 406 in Jerusalem. The

Frank in Palestine (1946)

company stayed in Jerusalem for ten months from where they carried out a number of operations. Frank went down to the Dead Sea, to Amman in Jordan and saw a considerable part of the country – although much of his time was spent helping to police the city.

It was not easy work because the soldiers never knew who their enemy was and where they were hiding. The city was divided into sections, including Russian and German compounds. The Sixth guarded the station, Barclays Bank, the YMCA and the King David Hotel. The High Commissioner's house seemed well policed already, having about three hundred and fifty guards on duty day and night. One night, when they were guarding the hotel, the enemy must have crept in the back way while the British were out the front because the building suddenly exploded. During the night Frank often went down to the Palestinian Police Headquarters to help patrol Jerusalem during the hours of darkness. The police had an armoured wireless car they used for keeping watch on the streets of the city and some outlying areas. The British vehicle, carrying five men and a driver, would follow the car looking for signs of trouble.

Whilst in Jerusalem the soldiers were each given a week's leave. They had the choice of visiting Cyprus or Cairo and Frank decided he would like to see Egypt. He travelled by train and found there was no glass in the windows, only shutters. But although he saw the Pyramids and other sights he did not enjoy his seven days in Cairo. It was dry, dusty and the culture seemed very foreign. When the troops in Jerusalem needed extra vehicles this also meant a trip to Egypt, to a place called Telekabir. Frank went with his unit across the desert on the train which stopped at the Suez Canal. One of the British Naval ships was passing down the canal at the time and the soldiers and sailors were close enough to be able to talk to each other. The sailors asked the men if they would like any cigarettes and when the soldiers eagerly said they would, they threw down tins of fifty from the decks. When the ship had passed the bridge was closed and the soldiers rushed to get back on the train.

From Jerusalem the soldiers would sometimes go to Bethlehem, and from there down the old road to the Dead Sea. Here, you could float on the amazingly salty water and read a book. A handful of water immediately became a handful of salt in the hot sun.

When they travelled through the desert the men stopped for the night and, no matter how remote the location, it seemed that within twenty

Palestine - MT section (Frank is top left)

minutes an Arab salesman would appear with his camel to show his wares. Frank was seeing a very different way of life and a great deal of the country as he transported people and goods here and there.

One day, an officer requested a vehicle to take sixteen men down to a police station in Jerusalem. Frank was, by this time, a Transport Sergeant. He had taken over from Vic Dowley who had now left the army and Vic, in his turn, had taken over from Sergeant Owen when he had been demobbed. The sixteen men were already in the back of the lorry when Frank climbed into the cab. He drove to the police station where he got out and unlatched the tailgate. What a surprise – the first man to get down from the lorry was George Parsons from Combe Road in Stonesfield. Frank asked, "What are you doing here then, George?"

"I've just been posted here," replied the young man, for whom it was his first time abroad.

As it happened Frank was to spend some time with George whose company sent him on an MT course so that he could drive one of their vehicles. But although Frank taught the young soldier to drive, when George got home he never drove again.

While Frank was in Palestine he caught pneumonia. He was taken to be treated in a hospital in Sarafan, and then, when he was recovering, sent to convalesce in Nathania. During his weeks' stay he tried to stay active and build up his strength. One day the patients decided a football game would be a good idea and decided to get two teams together. They saw a man running around on his own and asked him if he would like to join in.

"Yes," he said, "I don't mind."

The man chose to play up in the forward line and he turned out to be a very good player.

Someone said, "You've played before, haven't you?"

He said yes, he had played a bit. Later, the men found out that his name was Manion and he played for Middlesbrough.

After a short while back in Camp 406, Frank left Palestine on November 8th 1946. The company went up into Egypt and caught a boat, the Monarch of Bermuda, at Alexandria two days later. On November 19th they arrived at Southampton. A few days later Sergeant Hall arrived in Stonesfield for his sister's wedding. Emmie had declared there could be no wedding until Frank got home. Her father was almost blind and everyone agreed that Frank should give her away in his place. It was a good day. A happy time was had by all; Frank was home to stay. His time in the army was due to come to an end in March 1947 but he was allowed to stay at home on full pay until then. A remarkable and unforgettable chapter in his young life was drawing to a close.

It was good to be back at home with his family, but Frank was unsure what he wanted to do next. However, the winter of 1946-47 was one of the worst that anyone could remember and he was soon needed. It was 'all hands on deck' to keep village roads passable.

14

Frank had left behind him temperatures of up to 110 degrees F so his first three months back home were quite a shock. Snow fell steadily until the village was enveloped in a thick, white blanket. Down the hill that is still now The Ridings it drifted against a cottage so heavily that

Village working party, winter 1947

only the bedroom window was visible. The villagers left their work – they could not get there anyway – and set to, to reach the old couple who lived in the house. After two days' constant digging the men finally freed the back door and the old folk were released from their own home. Going down the road from the Victorian tap on the bend was like walking through a bright, white tunnel.

The snow did not thaw and so the digging had to go on. Every day someone would say, "I haven't seen old so-and-so for a couple of days. We'd better see if he wants digging out!"

It was a slow job: two or three days to dig to the North Leigh turn; a day and a half to get to the bottom of Combe Road and three or four days from the village to Black's Gate, set in the wall of the Blenheim Palace grounds. The first two or three weeks of the snow were quite chaotic. Even people who worked on the surrounding land had difficulty in getting to work and the owners of the glove factories in Woodstock realised quickly that they would not see many of their staff for some time.

After Frank had been back home for three months the weather was better, the Army had finished paying him and he needed a job. By chance, a Stonesfield man, Alec Harris, bumped into Frank one day and asked what he was doing. Alec had been in the Air Force and since his discharge had bought himself a lorry. He was using this to make deliveries for the Oxfordshire Farmers because although the committee had their own lorries they still needed more and his relation, farmer Freddie Whitlock, a member, had offered him this opportunity. Alec was kept very busy fetching and carrying and wondered if Frank could help him out for two or three days?

"Yes, I don't mind," said Frank.

The farmers had a small store in Walton Street in Oxford, but most of the supplies were kept in buildings rented from the Duke of Marlborough. Trains brought the goods into Woodstock station and Alec and Frank picked them up from there, taking them to be stored in what was called the Cow Yards on the palace estate. Later they would deliver what was needed out to the farms.

Alec's 'two or three days' became about twelve months, by which time he had started a new project. For a number of years Alec's brother had run a fish and chip shop in Bicester and had recently suggested to Alec that they start a mobile fish and chip round, to be operated by him and his wife. Alec thought this was a good idea and was soon driving the new van over from Stonesfield to collect the fish and chips each day except Mondays. On Tuesdays the van called at Wootton and Glympton; Wednesdays were spent serving the villagers in Stonesfield; Fawler and Finstock saw the van on Thursdays; on Fridays Alec called at Combe, Bladon and Hanborough. But Alec's wife had other things to do on Fridays and did not want to accompany him so Frank was asked if he would take her place. Frank agreed and every Friday he would finish working with the lorry by noon and be ready to join Alec on the fish and chip van in the evening. If he had time he drove to Bicester in his car to fetch the fish and chips but he needed to be back in the village by 3.30pm so that the two could start frying and be on the road by 4 o'clock.

Although Hanborough was next to Combe the van had to visit Bladon first. For some reason Hanborough had to be the last call so it was at least ten by the time the round was finished. One Friday evening in Bladon turned out to be very memorable for Frank. The van usually

Bladon, showing the Lamb public house (1959) (Photo: Oxford Mail and Times)

stopped near a pub called The Lamb and on this particular evening a young woman came out of the door to buy fish and chips. But the van had just moved off. The girl hurried back in and got out her bicycle. She was relieved to find the fish and chip van just along the road. She got off her bike and asked the good-looking young man inside for fish and chips. Frank liked the look of her and started a conversation. Her name was Jean, she was eighteen years old and lived with her family at The Lamb. She worked in the village in her uncle's grocery shop. Soon the pair were getting along like a house on fire.

After a few weeks' chatting like this Frank began to cycle over to Bladon and following a drink in the bar he and Jean would go across the road, through the iron gate and into Blenheim Park where they could walk around the lake and wander the beautiful grounds for as long as they liked. They could walk from Bladon to Combe or to Woodstock without touching a public road.

On Tuesdays and Thursdays coaches started off in Long Hanborough to collect people from the villages for a trip to the cinema in Kidlington. Oliver's used to do the Tuesday outings and Slatter's operated on a Thursday. The cinema (now a supermarket) was a very popular place and every Thursday Frank and Jean would catch separate buses and meet on the cinema steps. The cinema was always packed with people but because the Bladon bus arrived first Jean had already bought the tickets and as soon as Frank stepped off his bus the couple could go in and choose their seats without joining the queue. After the film and newsreels seven or eight coaches stood in the car park waiting to deliver people back to their homes.

Frank always went to church on Sundays but in the afternoon he would cycle over to Bladon for tea with Jean's family and another walk in the park. At that time the bridge over the lake had a gate at each end to keep the sheep and cattle to their own sides. One Sunday the young couple stood on the bridge looking down at the water when they saw a car approaching. To be helpful they opened the gate to let the car through and were thanked through the window by the Duke of Marlborough and Princess Margaret who had been spending the weekend there.

Frank and Jean on Bladon bridge (1950)

Percy Hall holding the cup. (1950s) (Photo: Oxford Mail and Times)

So Frank, now courting regularly, settled back into village life. Most evenings were spent at home and, in the summer, playing cricket, football or working on the allotment. Saturday afternoons were also spent playing cricket or football, depending on the season. Grampy Bill had now passed away and Frank's father, Percy, had come to live in the house. His sight was failing badly when he arrived and soon he became completely blind.

Even so, Percy had always been a gardener and worked outside on the farm. Soon he was working no less than three allotments and, for a while, five. He had looked after Frank's plot during the war but now his son was back home and could work alongside him. Gardening took all his time and interest. One allotment was given over to potatoes, another to greens and a third to parsnips, carrots, onions, beetroot – all the root vegetables. The family never had to buy a vegetable. On one of the plots Percy erected a little tin shed. Inside this he put bales of straw to keep out the frost and this made an excellent store for the potatoes. Through the year broad beans were followed by spring cabbage, May Queen broccoli that took a whole year to grow, summer cabbage and runner beans and peas, purple sprouting and Brussels sprouts, January King cabbage and savoys. Then the cycle would start all over again. He gave away some of the vegetables but most were soon eaten by the family of eight.

Percy worked on his allotments all day but in the summer, when the weather was hot, he took to working at night. On a warm day Frank often found him sat under the wall either asleep or smoking his pipe.

"You're not working then, Dad?" Frank would ask.

"Oh no," said Percy, "I started at two this morning, there's no need to work out in the sun."

Dark or light, it made no difference to him. He grew very good vegetables. For two years he was runner-up in the Stonesfield Flower Show and then won the cup for the following two. Emmy's husband Ken had come down from London and set up the vegetables for Percy who by this time could see nothing at all. It was something to be proud of and the local newspaper ran a report but soon after this the annual show was discontinued.

15

By 1949 Alec was getting fed up with the lorry work and decided to concentrate on the fish and chip round. Frank wanted to keep the job and fortunately Oxfordshire Farmers offered to employ him. He drove one of their vehicles, a Commer 2-stroke, registration OWL 709. Bernard Hunt let him keep the lorry in his farm yard. Every week saw him driving to Middlesex, Rotherhithe, Tilbury docks and down to Spillers in Avonmouth where he dropped off wheat to be milled into flour. Here he would pick up cow cake or pig food from another firm in the dock area and return with a loaded lorry.

Once a week Frank had a very early start and fetched the vehicle from the yard at three in the morning. If it was a Monday it was extra hard because he would have been over in Bladon courting Jean the previous evening. When the clock struck 12 he left Jean, jumped on his bike and cycled back to Stonesfield. Falling into bed he slept for a couple of hours before getting up and picking up the lorry. He drove to Kidlington where, at 3.30am, his mate Tom Bosher had a cup of tea waiting at his house in Evans Lane. The two drank their tea (Tom's always had four teaspoons of sugar in it) and then left for London.

The people working in the office in Beaumont Street in Oxford did not know London at all. If Frank and Tom had followed instructions to the letter they would have been driving from one side of the city to the other on routes that wasted much of their time and fuel. So the two men called for their orders and worked out between them the most economical ways to pick up calves' milk substitute from Middlesex, kibbled maize for chickens at Rotherhithe and tons of supplies from Tilbury docks.

One Monday morning Frank left home at three and made his way via White City, Shepherd's Bush, Fulham embankment, over the bridge and through the Rotherhithe tunnel to the Elephant and Castle and down to the docks. Here, he loaded ten tons of fertiliser onto the lorry. He drove back to Oxfordshire where he delivered the load to Nuneham Courtenay. After unloading the fertiliser he piled ten tons of wheat onto the now empty vehicle. This was destined for Avonmouth so he was soon back on the road driving west. Having delivered the wheat Frank crossed the docks to pick up ten tons of cattle cake before he returned to Oxfordshire. He arrived in Stonesfield at nine in the evening, very tired. His working week, including unpaid overtime and Saturday mornings, was usually between seventy and eighty hours long. The pay was £5-11s a week.

One Christmas Eve Frank drove through pouring rain to Avonmouth with two other drivers and their lorries. Waiting in the docks was a load of thirty tons. The smallest lorry, a seven-ton Austin, was loaded first and the driver went on his way. Frank and Tom Bosher loaded their vehicles and Tom was the next to leave. Frank's cattle cake was needed urgently by a farmer in Middle Barton and Tom said that when he had delivered his own load he would come to the farm and help Frank finish his unloading. At nearly 7 o'clock in the evening the two men were working hard, and by now the rain was soaking their clothes. There were 160 bags of cow cake in a ten-ton load and eventually all were stacked in the barn. As Frank and Tom were covering the back of the lorry and tying up the ropes the farmer came along.

"Right, I've put your Christmas box on the back of your lorry," he said, indicating Tom's vehicle. "Have a good Christmas."

The two men thanked him very much and when the sheets were all tidied up went round to the back of Tom's lorry. There, sitting smooth and round, were two hen's eggs – one each. The men looked at each other and decided it was time they went home to change their sodden clothes.

It was usually quite late in the day when Frank arrived back in Oxfordshire and one day he drove into Park Farm in Combe at five in the evening. Again, on the lorry were ten tons of Avonmouth cattle cake. Frank knew Walter Green, the farmer, and his crew very well and caught sight of Bill Clack who drove the farm lorry. Bill strolled over and asked what Frank was delivering today. When Frank told him he had 160 sacks Bill said, "Well, we can't help you Frank, because we don't get any overtime paid after 5 o'clock."

With that the men all got out their bicycles and pedalled off home. Walter came out of the farmhouse and asked what was on the lorry.

"I've got your ten tons of cow cake, Mr Green," replied Frank. "Where do you want it put?"

Walter took him along to the barns. Although Walter's son and grandson are still busy to this day with contract work, the barns have been mostly converted to other uses. One of these buildings still has at least a dozen steps leading up to the door and this was the one where the cake was to be stored.

So at 5 o'clock Frank started carrying the sacks up the steps and one hundred and sixty journeys and two hours later he was finished. He was never paid a penny in overtime. He was getting fed up with the whole thing. Calling with a load at Busby's in Combe at 7 o'clock one evening, Frank asked for a hand unloading.

"Oh no," said Mr Busby, "we don't work after 5 o'clock."

"That's alright then," said Frank, "I'll come at 7 o'clock in the morning."

The man was surprised – he thought Frank was well-paid and earned extra money for evening work. Frank was equally surprised that the man, who belonged to Oxfordshire Farmers, did not know how little he received for his long working week. He suggested that next time he went to a meeting he brought the matter up. But matters did not improve and Frank and Tom had had enough. Frank said, "I think I shall look for another job."

Tom agreed with the idea and said he would too. It was 1949 and there was plenty of work about.

Frank got talking to an acquaintance in Freeland village shortly afterwards and the man told him that Bert Dix, the sand and gravel extractor, could do with some drivers.

So Frank knew that it would be quite easy to find something new. He drove into the farmers' office in Oxford and asked the secretary if he could speak to Mr Scott, the manager. She said he was busy, but Frank insisted and was called up to Mr Scott's office. The manager asked what was the matter.

"Well, we're looking for some more money," Frank told him. "We work 70 or 80 hours a week and no overtime. I wondered if you could pay us a bit more?"

"Dear oh dear," said Mr Scott, "You'll soon want as much as we're getting!"

"But we're doing the work!" exclaimed the young man.

The manager told him no, there was no way they could pay him any more.

"Oh well," said Frank "then I'll finish – now. I'll come in on Friday and pick my wages up."

Mr Scott was horrified and said he could not do this.

"Yes I can," said Frank, "if you won't pay me any more. I'll find another job."

"What's going to happen to the lorry then?" asked Mr Scott.

The office was in Beaumont Street, next to the Oxford Playhouse. Frank had parked the lorry next to the theatre. He answered, "I don't know – it's your lorry."

With that he left the office, walked round to the bus station at Gloucester Green and caught a bus to Stonesfield.

Back in the village, Frank got his bike out and cycled up to Dix's place in Freeland where he got off his bike and walked up the drive. A man coming towards him asked,

"Can I help you?"

"I'm looking for Mr Dix," said Frank.

"I am Mr Dix," came the reply. "What are you looking for?"

Frank told him he was looking for a job.

"Have you done much driving?" asked Bert Dix.

"Oh yes," said Frank and told him all about his driving during the war and since. Bert wanted to know what was wrong with Oxfordshire Farmers?

"Too little pay and too long hours," replied the ex-employee.

But when he learned that Frank was paid £5-11s a week Mr Dix told him that he could only pay £4-15s. Frank was not too worried about that and found out that the hours would be 7am to 5pm, five and a half days a week. Mr Dix thought he might not be happy with the early

A Dix lorry dropping off its load (1961) (Photo: Oxford Mail and Times)

mornings as 7am was the time the lorries must leave the yard so in reality the drivers needed to be there earlier. But to someone who had been getting out of bed at half-past three this was no problem. It was agreed that Frank would go home and think about things and if he wanted the job he would start the following Monday.

As he cycled home he mulled over the conversation. Once home he thought about what it would mean. He had been getting £5-11s for up to 80 hours a week. He would now be working from 7am to 5pm; he would be going down to the pit where the lorry would be loaded by machine; there would be no long-distance driving; he would open the tailboard at his destination and the material would pour out. He compared it with his old job of very long hours and very long journeys; of loading and unloading sack after heavy sack on his back. And he thought, well, that'll do me.

So Frank went back to Freeland and told Bert Dix that he would start on Monday. It was August, 1950.

At first the new job was steady and uneventfully busy. Oxfordshire was rich in gravel and a good number of firms were in the business at that time. As well as G. H. Dix there were Sands and Gravels, Partridges, Tuckwells, Curtiss and John Brown from Hanborough. Bert Dix had three brothers working with him. Bert was in overall charge. His elder brother, Stan, was foreman of the Stanton Harcourt pit. Brother Cyril drove the lorries and kept a watchful eye on them while younger brother, Peter, drove the navvy that dug the gravel out of the pit. It was a growing business but the following year it really exploded.

1951 saw the US Airforce moving in and taking over Upper Heyford and Brize Norton bases. With a sudden need for much longer runways the local gravel industry was overwhelmed and had to have help from farther afield. Bert bought a new Priestman Tiger for Peter which only needed three draglines to fill a lorry instead of the ten that their Priestman Cubs needed. It seemed that everything was going from small to large within weeks. Next to arrive were two new Leyland Comets, six-yarders instead of four and the cat's whiskers of the transport world. It was, of course, quite natural for Cyril Dix to have one of these but then Frank was very pleased to be asked if he would like the other. Apart from a short break when he had to return to Tidworth army base for 'Reserve training', Frank drove the big vehicle from November to March the following year.

One day during that month Frank was in the yard when the manager, a Mr Holmes, approached him and said, "We shall have to finish you, Frank."

"Why, what's the matter?" asked Frank.

"Oh nothing really," said the manager, "but we've got to cut down on one or two drivers so we thought you'd have to go."

So Frank had to leave his job and go home. This was not good; he and Jean were going to be married the following week.

16

On March 29th 1952 the bridegroom woke up to a very cold morning. Although temporarily out of work, Frank knew something would turn up and was determined to enjoy his wedding.

Frank with brothers-in-law Les and Don

The first thing to be done was to collect the flowers from Carterton. It had been arranged that Charlie Dore would take Frank over in his car at ten o'clock. Just before the hour the groom walked down Churchfields to the yard where Charlie was waiting with his long-nosed Morris to take him over to the nurseries. As they left the village a few snowflakes drifted onto the car windscreen. Frank was pleased with the flowers, especially Jean's bouquet of red roses. He paid the nurseryman ten pounds – a reduction for cash – and Charlie turned the car round and drove back to Stonesfield.

By this time it was snowing steadily and cold as winter. Frank's brother-in-law, Les Baldwin, had agreed to be Best Man and by the time Frank met him off the Worth's bus Les had already had a couple of nips from the bottle of whisky he had brought with him. The two men warmed up at home and settled down to wait for Charlie who would be arriving with the car at ten minutes to two.

But the time came and went and there was no sign of Charlie. Five more minutes passed and Frank, rather worried by now, said to Les, "We'd better go down and see where he is!"

When Charlie had come back from Carterton he had parked the Morris tight against the closed garage doors in an attempt to keep it free from snow. Unfortunately, when he had tried to start the engine the starter had jammed. Frank and Les found him very agitated and swearing at the useless vehicle. The two men rocked the car back and forth and eventually the engine spluttered to life.

They all jumped in the car and Charlie put his foot down. Frank had invited Bernard Fowler to the wedding and had offered him a lift to

March 29, 1952

Bladon. Bernard walked up from his house in the Combe road and waited by the engine yard. By the time the car finally rounded the bend the poor man, who was dressed for the wedding and wore no overcoat, was covered in snow and chilled to the bone. Frank bundled him into the back seat and Charlie roared off. Time was getting short; the wedding was at half-past two and it was well after 2 o'clock already. When they got to the junction with the main road to Woodstock

Charlie startled the passengers by taking the right turn without slowing or stopping.

"We haven't got time!" he shouted when the men commented on this risky action.

The car pulled into Bladon at twenty past two in a blizzard. Although Frank was very relieved to arrive on time and in one piece, a few people thought he looked frightened. It was not fear that made him look pinched and pale but the intense cold which, after trying to start the car in the yard and a journey in the same unheated vehicle, had really penetrated all the travellers. It was good to get into the church where about fifty friends and family members were waiting to see the young couple take their vows.

The wedding reception was held in the church room, by the lych gate. Hall's of Eynsham were the caterers and they gave a bowl of Christmas pudding to each of the wedding guests as they entered the room. It was a warm welcome on such a day. A month previously, on February 23rd, Jean's sister Barbara had been married on a glorious day that felt like summer. Frank and Jean's wedding day would be remembered as a day when spring slipped back into winter, but the warmth and happiness of the occasion soon enveloped all the guests and a very good time was had by all.

In the evening the young couple left for Marston in Oxford. Jean's stepsister had given them the keys to her home as she would be away for the weekend. There was one small condition attached: one of her friends from Marston would be attending the wedding and would need a lift home with Frank and Jean. That was fine, so at 7 o'clock Frank gave a nod to Chick Fowler who was driving and the newlyweds, along with Doris, left for Oxford. All went well until they got to Wolvercote level crossing where the gates were closed. They sat for a while watching railway wagons shunting back and forth, Doris sitting alongside Chick in the front seat. Meanwhile the drifting snow was building up and when the gates opened the car's wheels started to spin. Chick tried hard not to dig in deeper as he did all he could to get the car moving. For a while the four of them thought they would be stuck but eventually, after a bit of shunting of his own, Chick managed to drive off.

They dropped off Doris first. Stopping outside her house and helping her out of the car, Frank realised that she had had a little too much to drink at the reception. He managed to find her front door key in her handbag and carefully walked her to the front door. Opening the door, Frank saw the stairs immediately in front of him. What could he do with this lady who was rather 'worse for wear'? He led her inside, leant her against the wall near the bottom step, set her handbag beside her and quietly closed the front door behind him. They hoped she would be all right. Jean's stepsister said later that Doris had no recollection of coming home and was worried that she had spoiled things. But a few weeks later everyone met up again at the Marlborough hotel where the two ladies worked and they all had a good laugh.

Frank and Jean spent the weekend at Marston. On Monday it was Jean's birthday and then time for her to go back to work at the shop in Bladon. For Frank it was time to look for a job.

He had heard that CSE, the aviation people at Kidlington airfield, were looking for someone. In 1952 this was the home of the University Air Squadron. They flew Chipmunks and were based here for pilot training. There was no proper runway at the aerodrome, just a wide area of grass. Frank was employed with another worker to watch the men and the planes and be on hand to act quickly in any emergency. Each morning they would drive out a fire engine and an ambulance and park them on the field. The rest of the day was spent in a shed from where they could watch the training – jumping into one of the vehicles should it become necessary.

He was earning a wage but Frank missed the driving that had occupied him since his army days. After twelve months he had had enough of the job and wanted to move on. He bumped into Bill Kitchin, a workmate from Dix's, who seemed to be pleased with his new job at Sidney Smart's at Cokethorpe, near Witney. Sidney Smart had bought a hay and straw business from B. T. Frost, the coal merchant. For a while Mr Frost had run the threshers alongside his coal business but he decided he no longer wanted them. So he sold the business to Mr Smart, along with eight or nine lorries that were used to deliver the threshed hay and straw far and wide. Bill drove one of these lorries and Frank decided to join him.

Smart's delivered hay to Birmingham and Coventry police for their horses and to racing stables in Fulham, London. Sturgeon's in Liverpool also wanted the hay for their race horses and it was usually sent up there by rail. In addition, Frank and the other drivers would sometimes deliver ten or fifteen loads of straw to Charlbury or Hanborough station. In those days straw was widely used for all kinds of things. It was needed by glass makers like Pilkington's in their packing departments; by Dolton's pipe packers who wove it into ropes and wound it round the huge tubes for transportation. Frank used to drive down to Eely paper mills, beyond Cardiff, where the straw was used in the manufacture of cardboard. It was a busy life and he enjoyed it far more than his previous job. But after a year with Smart's he happened to meet Ken Bint from Northmoor, another of his mates from Dix's.

"How's it going then, Ken?" asked Frank.

Ken looked less than pleased. There had been a bit of friction in the firm and it centred round Peter Dix. At first Peter had enjoyed operating the huge Priestman Tiger but after a while he was getting bored with it and wanted to drive a lorry. And the lorry he wanted to drive was Frank's Leyland Comet. This was the reason why Frank had lost his job. When the rest of the workforce found out they were not happy and there was a lot of grumbling which eventually reached the ears of Bert Dix. It had been going on for some months already and was to rumble on for another two or three.

After this time the two men bumped into each other again and Ken told Frank that Dix's were looking for some more drivers. Did he ever think about coming back?

"Well, I don't know," said Frank.

He thought about it, decided it would be an easier job than the one he had and plucked up the courage to walk back up the drive and see Mr Dix. Bert asked him straight away, "Are you looking for a job then, Frank?"

"Well, I don't know", said Frank again. "Somebody said you were looking for some more drivers?"

The reply was immediate: "Start when you like Frank. And you can have your old lorry back."

Peter was no longer working with the firm. Amey's, the gravel producer from Wootton, near Abingdon, was about to start work on the M1 motorway. They knew that he was used to the Tiger and offered him a job driving a big machine for them. Peter was unable to resist the offer and had gone to work on the new road.

Frank was very pleased to be back in his job.

17

Jean had been born at The Lamb in Bladon and for the first twelve months of their married life she and Frank lived there with the family. Jean went back to her job which was now across the road at Walford's, a very busy grocer's and baker's shop serving Bladon and delivering to the surrounding villages in a number of Commer vans. At the end of the year the young couple moved up to 21 Heath Lane where they shared a four-bedroom council house with Jean's sister and her husband. It was here that their first child, Stephen, was born. Quite soon number 33, a two-bedroom house opposite, became vacant and the family moved into a home of their own.

The family at Heath Lane (1955)

Well settled in Bladon, the couple joined in local activities and attended the village church. Frank joined the British Legion soon after he arrived and became involved in all the meetings, outings and the annual sale of poppies. It was not long before he was back to bell-ringing. Unlike Stonesfield there were no bells ringing out from St Martin's on Sundays;

Stephen and Rosemary (1962)

they had been silent here for years. An ex-soldier, Oddie Danbury, a man left with only one leg after the war, had been a bell-ringer until 1939. He approached Frank one day and said, "You ring bells don't you, Frank? Do you think we could start up here again?"

Frank agreed that, yes, he had been ringing at Stonesfield and he thought it would be a good idea. They put a notice in the church magazine to attract some interest and gradually the Bladon bells started to call the villagers to church twice every Sunday. Over the next few years Oddie and Frank trained fifteen ringers.

In January 1961 the cottage belonging to the church became vacant and was offered to Frank and Jean. In return for a rent-free home and the sum of ten shillings a week, Frank, in the position of Verger, was to look after the outside of the church while his wife cared for the inside. The previous occupant, Stan Kingsbury, had lived on his own in Church Cottage and when the Halls moved in the place had an air of neglect. Stan had changed the oil from his motorbike in the front room and there was a lot of scrubbing and cleaning to be done. Even when the cottage was clean and painted the facilities remained very basic with the lavatory at the bottom of the garden. But the family made the best of things and soon they had another new member; Stephen's sister Rosemary was born later that year.

Frank and Jean worked hard. As well as the church building they were also expected to keep the church room clean and tidy. Jean, on her hands and knees, used to scrub the whole of the wooden floor of this large room that had held their wedding guests.

The church was none too clean when the couple took it over and the grass in the churchyard rarely cut. Behind the church the area was

The parish church of St Martin (1962)

completely overgrown and Frank, starting work with a scythe, spent most of his evenings and weekends cutting and clearing the tangled wilderness. Inside the building the walls were dark and grubby; the wooden floor wobbly and uneven. But Frank and Jean worked with what they had and the church and churchyard gradually took on the look of a place that people cared about.

During the winter months, on Saturday afternoons, Frank took up to twenty-four buckets of coal across to the church. This was stored below ground level and used to start the boiler beneath the gratings. On cold Sundays the ladies would stand over these gratings and take comfort from the warmth rising over their chilled feet and legs and creeping inside their coats and skirts. Every Saturday afternoon Frank burned some wood on the fire and when it had caught nicely, piled on some coal followed by anthracite. He could not go far because he had to come back after an hour to build up the fire again. A pipe led from the fire to the top of the tower where the flue came out.

If the weather had been wet this could cause real problems. Coming back to stoke up the fire, Frank would open the door to the church and find the building full of thick, dark smoke and the fire dead. The flue was too damp to dry out and the smoke could not get through. A sooty film glued itself to the pews and needed to be removed by the following morning. Jean would bring damp cloths and the pair had to wipe every pew clean before they started to polish them. It was not unusual for Frank and Jean to fall into bed at midnight at times like this. Even then there was

Frank mowing by Sir Winston's grave

no time for a full night's sleep. The old stove had a crack in it and Frank used to walk over at about two in the morning to stoke up the fire, followed by another visit at six. It was a time- consuming operation and the boiler was not very efficient but without it the church would have been very cold indeed.

But a big change was to come about for St Martin's. This church that was struggling to make ends meet was soon to become much more wealthy, and all thanks to the man the nation had relied upon during the war. The great Sir Winston Churchill would be laid to rest in this little country churchyard, and the people were generous in their appreciation.

A few months before Winston's death in January 1965, Frank had bumped into a man holding a little boy's hand as they walked through the churchyard. The man introduced himself as Richard Dimbleby; the little boy was either David or Jonathan. He had explained to Frank that Winston's health was failing, he would be buried here and the BBC were hoping to cover the event. Like the professional he was he wanted to get a feel for the church and surroundings beforehand. As soon as the death was announced all kinds of people began to arrive in Bladon. During the week before the funeral Peter Dimmock came in his capacity as Head of Outside Broadcasting. As Frank busied himself tidying and preparing the churchyard for the burial he was constantly interrupted by cries of, "Where's Frank?"

Mr Dimmock relied on Frank for his knowledge of the church and village and needed his help in stopping the church clock at three so that cameras could film the hands pointing to the time of the funeral. The bells were going to be rung by the Launton bell-ringers who were regarded as a highly professional team. Frank met with the man in charge of this, a Mr Sharp, to arrange a day when all the bells, their

The BBC arrive in Bladon (Photo: Oxford Mail and Times)

slides and stays could be checked. A plaque in the church tower records the names of all the ringers and the man in charge of the peal, a Mr Wigg, the names of the Rector and the two Churchwardens. Photographers from all parts of the world started to appear in the village. Whilst Frank and Mr Sharp were in discussion by the lych gate an American lady, slung with cameras, interrupted them and persuaded Mr Sharp to let her treat him to lunch at The Bear Hotel in Woodstock where she could ask him more about church bells.

The County Council was worried that the weather would turn frosty and salted all the roads from Hanborough station to Bladon church. It could not afford any problems for the cortege and the thirteen following Rolls Royces. Frank was the one who had the problem later when the crowds of people trampled in the salt and onto the grass inside the roped-off area of the path, turning it to mud. In the early morning he would have to hose down the concrete path, doing his best to clean it.

After the pomp and ceremony of his funeral in London, Sir Winston Churchill's body was taken by train to Hanborough station and driven from there to Bladon where he was buried in the churchyard. It was a Saturday. The only 'civilian' at the graveside was Frank Hall, the Verger. Winston's wife, Clementine, had told the BBC that she wanted this last episode to be private but the police did not quite know for certain how this was to be interpreted. The BBC and all their paraphernalia were camped over the wall of the churchyard in the adjoining school playground. They stayed there, hoping they would be able to film parts of the country funeral, until midnight on Friday but the police decided to close everything off at the lych gate.

Seventy-five officers had been sent to police Bladon and they spread out in rings around the village centre. Sharp eyes had already spotted

Crowds wait to pay their respects (Photo: Oxford Mail and Times)

photographers from *Paris Match* perched in trees, their long lenses at the ready. The police needed to be very vigilant. The village was closed at ten on Saturday morning and the public began their long wait to show their respects to the great man.

After the burial the grave was filled. The media were impatient. An important-looking policeman called Smith darted back and forth between Frank's group of helpers and the lych gate by Church Cottage.

"How long are you going to be before you've got that grave filled in?" he kept asking.

Frank said they were working as fast as they could and Inspector Smith said he would wait for a 'thumbs up' sign. But waiting with the group of pushing, eager photographers was difficult. Glancing towards the grave he saw the new mound of earth and thought it really must be time now. Frank had to stop him opening the gates before the wreaths, beginning with those of Clementine and the Queen, were arranged on the ground in the proper manner.

At last it was done, Frank gave him the sign and the dam of photographers burst through the gates. They were allowed just ten chaotic minutes to take their pictures before being ushered out by the police. Most co-operated, but one, a fellow with a bandaged head, had not managed to take his photos in the crush and was now busily clicking away by the graveside. He was soon spotted and two policeman lifted him up, swiftly depositing him over the wall into the school yard. As soon as they had their photographs the reporters rushed across the road to the White House public house. Here they were able to send off their reports by telephone using one of the six temporary phone boxes which had been installed next to the existing village box.

When the press were out of the way the police opened the gates to the public. The people filed past the grave in their thousands and it was not until 2 o'clock on Sunday morning that there was any sign of a slowing down. The grave was floodlit during the hours of darkness. This was a help when the wreaths were taken off and laid in the aisle of the church. At 5am people started coming into the churchyard again, the wreaths were soon replaced after the threat of frost had passed and the queue was continuous for another twenty-four hours. Church services took place as usual. The police helped the villagers get through the crowds to the church but one frail old lady was still accused of jumping the queue when she tried to go to Evensong. In the vestry door was a small slot into which people could put donations. Behind the slot was a box the size of two or three matchboxes. Frank had always emptied the box and taken out the few coins.

This evening it was a different story. When Frank went into church the policeman on duty came up to him and said, "Frank, your box is full. The people can't get the money in and they're leaving it on the step!"

Frank collected the money and spoke with the church treasurer the following morning. They both agreed something had to be done. After some discussion Frank went to see Marsh Devonshire. This man used to be a baker in Stonesfield and had moved to Rectory Farm in Bladon. Frank had thought a flour sack, which would be tightly woven, could be the answer to their problem and asked if he could borrow one. The baker agreed and the sack was hooked onto a wicker chair behind the vestry door. Money poured through the slot in the door. Twice a day for the next week Frank emptied the sack into two buckets and took the money to the treasurer's house. The man and his wife spent their days doing nothing but counting this money which they paid into the bank three times a day. After a few months the donations had amounted to somewhere between £12,000 and £13,000.

During this time the grave was guarded at night by two policemen. Officers were drafted in from all over Oxfordshire. Every night at ten Frank and Jean would call them into the church room to get warm by the old Tortoise stove and Jean would make toast and a cup of cocoa. Cups and saucers, tea and milk were left in the room along with a few glasses and a bottle of whisky. The weather was cold and the couple's kindness was appreciated. After it was all over and things had quietened down they were given a pair of brass candlesticks by Inspector Jeacock of Woodstock, to express the thanks of the force.

Cameras roll as Senator Kennedy recalls a great statesman (Photo: Oxford Mail and Times)

Famous people came to pay their last respects to Sir Winston Churchill, among them Lord Mountbatten. A large limousine drew up and Senator Robert Kennedy climbed out, surrounded by his bodyguards. Frank and Jean had been told of this visit and waited outside Church Cottage while Mr Kennedy walked up to the grave. As usual the chauffeur turned the car round while he waited and and then held one of the doors open for the Senator. But on his return the Mr Kennedy walked behind the car towards the Halls with an outstretched hand.

"Nice to see you," he said. "How are you?"

The couple shook hands with him and chatted for a few minutes. Two or three reporters were watching every move and as soon as the Senator shook hands again, told Frank and Jean how nice it had been to meet them and departed, they rushed over for a blow-by-blow account of the conversation. It had been a very significant time to be living in Church Cottage.

18

At last St Martin's had the means to rectify some of its old problems. To Frank's relief the church council decided to spend some money on oil-fired heating. The next priority was decoration of the gloomy interior of the church followed soon by the replacement of the wobbly old floorboards with a new floor. At Church Cottage the family still used the lavatory at the bottom of the garden so another project was to install a proper bathroom with flush toilet.

Frank and Jean were very pleased with the alterations but they began to think of moving on. It was 1968, Frank had worked on the churchyard for seven years and it looked good. The church looked beautiful but they still seemed to spend every spare moment working. Frank was away from the house for twelve hours every day and when he got home there was always some church matter to deal with. Between them, he and Jean belonged to about thirteen committees which meant lots of meetings to attend. Frank was on the Parish Council and the Parochial Church Council, was Chairman of the Darts Club, helped with the local Youth Club along with Jean and looked after the two football teams. He felt it was time to leave Bladon, and his wife, who spent so much of her time cleaning in the church and the church room, agreed with him.

Frank was by this time working as a Rep. for Amey's and one of his contacts was a builder called Arthur Bowerman. Frank called on him one day while he was building some bungalows in Stonesfield. He liked the look of the two that were completed, backing onto fields off the Woodstock road. Arthur said he would have finished the third by the early part of 1969.

"Why don't you have it?"

Frank asked him how much it would cost and when Arthur suggested £5000 he made up his mind to buy it. He was sure Jean would want it too. Frank Hall was coming back to Stonesfield.

As well as the children, the family had an extra member. Jean's mother had been a widow since 1959 and now she came with her daughter and son-in-law to Stonesfield.

She lived with them until her death twenty-three years later. At first Jean worked in the glove factory that was now in the village in what used to be the back yard of The Crown public house. Also in the yard was Vic Griffin. He had built up a little business buying and selling secondhand furniture and he rented one of the barns for storage. Frank and Jean managed to find some bits and pieces there for the new bungalow. The glove factory belonged to Pickard's and Frank knew one or two of the workers from the village, but also one Claude Duval from Charlbury who had been a sergeant in the Ox and Bucks regiment with him. Claude played cricket for Ditchley park and Frank would play against him outside the big house when the Stonesfield team had a match there.

After a year or two Jean had to leave the factory to help Marion. Frank's sister had been running the Post Office in Churchfields along with Aunt Tilly. But Aunt Tilly had become too ill to work any longer so for the next fifteen years Jean took her place. When her mother became confined to a wheelchair in 1987 Jean left her work to look after her.

It was just before Frank's own retirement from ARC.

* * *

Frank had been a Rep. for the last twenty-three years of his working life but back in the fifties he was driving a lorry out from Dix pit. During the war this area had been an aerodrome for Bomber Command. When Frank started in 1950 there were still two runways and they were used as storage areas for materials. At first the gravel was being extracted at Blackditch but this supply was running out and digging started towards Standlake. Eventually, over the next few years, the concrete runway from Northmoor to Standlake was broken up and replaced by a haul road running by the river and around the site.

In 1958 G H Dix was taken over by Amey's. Later on Amey's bought out Associated Roadstone, based down in the west country, so becoming ARC – Amey Roadstone Company. This was part of the Consolidated Goldfield Group with goldmines in South Africa and tin mines in America. The company was to grow in size and importance.

The late fifties and early sixties were busy years for road builders. Work began on the M1, Britain's first motorway. Another gravel extractor, John Brown of Hanborough, had been hoping to buy some ground near the new road and invited Frank to join him and take charge of the six lorries he wanted to take there. Although that plan fell through, probably because the firm was too small to compete, John left the offer of a job permanently open to Frank.

Frank was happy where he was. Conbloc now belonged to Amey's and opened up a Premix plant on the site. It was an important operation and when the firm was working on the Heyford and Brize Norton runways it opened a huge asphalt plant. On some days there would be a hundred lorries running out of Stanton Harcourt through the narrow streets of the village of Eynsham up to the main A40 road where the drivers could pull in to the little café for a bacon sandwich before heading off north or west.

After ten years of lorry driving Frank had a change and worked for six years in the pit under Stan Dix, the foreman. But a bigger change followed this when he became a sales representative for the firm. He was given a Ford Anglia car and spent much of his time travelling around Oxfordshire, going north to the Banbury area, west to Carterton and Burford, down to Kingston Bagpuize and part of the city of Oxford as well as seeing clients in Buckingham and Brackley, Northants. One hundred and fifty customers, small builders and big, kept Frank very busy and as the Americans settled at Upper Heyford he found himself at the aerodrome seven or eight times a week.

The asphalt for the runways here had to come from carboniferous limestone, rather than the local, softer, oolitic limestone so this was sent from the west country at the rate of one thousand tons a day. Seventy-four shelters, called 'blisters', were built for the F1-11 planes and each shelter took one thousand metres of concrete which in turn needed two thousand tons of aggregate. Similar work was happening at the Brize Norton base for the Americans there. Many different building firms were involved so Frank, now photographed and issued with a security badge, seemed to be driving though one of the various gates around the airfields once, if not twice, a day. Later on the firm had a large contract with Keiran's to supply the materials for the building of the M40. Once again, three trains a day came up from Titherington, bringing limestone into Kidlington railhead (now Water Eaton Park and Ride area).

A Rep's job was to keep in touch with all his customers, hoping that by giving an efficient, friendly, personal service they would be loyal to the firm. Frank got to know all the builders from miles around and told them all that they could ring him any time from half-past six in the morning and during the evening if they needed anything. A builder would ring him at home before breakfast saying, "Frank, we've got a problem. I forgot to order some material and we've got a couple of bricklayers starting this morning – can you do anything for us?"

Frank would ring Fred at the weighbridge. Before he got the words out, Fred said,

"Yes, you want a favour then, don't you?"

Later in the morning a load of bricklaying sand was on its way to the builder.

One day a man called Jack Reed rang from Shilton needing sand for his bricklayers there. Frank rang Fred as usual but Fred said no, he was just too busy to supply them.

"Oh well," said Frank, "I'll just leave it with you then. See you later."

When he got to work after 8 o'clock, Frank asked Fred if he had had any luck with Jack's sand. As he spoke Sid, one of the drivers, walked through the door.

"Ask him," said Fred. "He's just delivered it."

The customers appreciated the extra effort and the business, now ARC, grew. Frank enjoyed the work and the contacts he made, and every two years he was given a new car. The Ford Anglia was followed by Morris Marinas and a Ford Cortina and, as Frank came nearer to retirement, Ford Escorts.

When the time came for Frank to finish work some of the smaller builders began to talk of leaving. Many felt things would be different when he had gone and they would probably take their custom elsewhere. Frank's colleague Alfie had left the Premix section and gone to work for Smith's sand and gravel firm. When Frank met up with him later Alfie confirmed that Smith's had indeed benefited from quite a number of new customers.

On his retirement, a few of his colleagues invited Frank and Jean to join them for a drink at one of the Witney pubs. When the couple arrived at half-past six the bar was quiet but Frank suddenly caught sight of Arthur Hunt (of Hunt and Townsend) with his wife.

"Well, fancy seeing you here!" said Frank.

"Yes, sorry we can't stop," replied Arthur, "but we've got another 'do' to go to. It would have been nice to see some of the other builders."

With that, Frank realised that more than just a drink had been arranged and although no longer a surprise, he and Jean went on to enjoy a very memorable evening with many friends.

When Arthur Hunt realised that he had spilled the beans he decided he would give Frank his gift of a clock there and then, on behalf of Hunt and Townsend. Other gifts followed when everyone else turned up, including a poem written by one of the girls in the office. It praised

Frank's contribution to all their lives and told how much they would miss him. So in 1988 life changed again for him and other interests had to fill the gap left by his working life.

19

When Frank came back to Stonesfield in 1969 after seventeen years the village felt quite different. Children he had grown up with were now married, some had left the area and some lived in the many new houses that had been built. Some of the shops had closed by now but Eric Hanks still had his bakery on the corner, his wife having a little shop selling odds and ends behind the deep bay window. In Churchfields the butcher's shop, Uncle Alf's shop and the Post Office were thriving although the Boot Street Post Office had closed. The little Salvation Army citadel was now a shop. Of the pubs The Crown, The Boot and the Maltshovel had closed leaving just The Black Head and The White Horse.

But soon the family settled down and began to feel at home. When the Halls lived at Bladon life had been hectic. One thing Frank and Jean were looking forward to was a break from all the committee meetings they had had to attend.

"Don't worry," Frank said to his wife, "nobody will know us after so long and we won't be doing anything."

But one job was already waiting for Frank in Stonesfield.

Before they left Bladon Major Duncan, the area officer for the British Legion, had come over from Taston to give him a certificate thanking him for all the work he had done for the Legion in the village. There was also another matter to discuss.

"I understand you're going to Stonesfield, Frank?" said the Major.

"Yes, that's right," replied Frank.

The officer explained that PC Wright, who had been organising the poppy collection there, was now moving to Wootton.

"I wondered if you could do it when you get to Stonesfield – just for this year? We'll find someone else to take it over, but if you could just do it this time I'd be grateful."

The 'someone else' was never found; Frank did the job for the next

Frank, Major Howard and Alfie Woodward (driver for 'C' company and a Bladon man) outside the Pegasus museum in 1987

forty years. He was always aware that the need for help did not stop with the soldiers of the first two wars but is still needed by the ex-servicemen and the families of the 32,000 killed since 1945.

Many of the smaller places like Combe, Freeland and Hanborough lost their British Legion branch as membership dwindled. Those still enthusiastic, like Frank, joined the larger Woodstock branch. In 1987 Frank went to France with the Legion on a trip to Normandy, and was reunited with Major Howard. The Major returned to France every year on the anniversary of the D-Day landings to talk about his war experiences with students and interested visitors.

In recent years the Woodstock branch has been invited to sell poppies at the Cherwell Valley service station on the M40 motorway and this has added about £6,000 a year to the local collections. Although Frank belonged to this branch with its committee and officers, he was the sole representative in Stonesfield. On handing in the money from the poppy sales there was a form to be completed. Frank's form had the following signatures - Chairman: F. Hall; Honorary Secretary: F. Hall; Treasurer: F. Hall. He kept a record of every penny ever collected; of every volunteer who helped; of every amount that each person collected.

Two weeks after the Halls moved into their new bungalow there came a knock on the door. Frank opened the front door and there stood a man who introduced himself as Bob Hain. He seemed to know all about Frank.

"You're Marion's brother aren't you?" said Bob. "I hear you've just moved from Bladon and been helping with the Youth Club there?"

Frank agreed with this and told Bob about looking after the football teams.

"Well," said Bob, we're looking for someone to help with the Youth Club here. I just wondered if..."

Frank hesitated a little so Bob told him to have a think about it.

He thought. Before long both Frank and Jean were on the Stonesfield Youth Club committee with Bob and Ginge West. Ginge was in charge and gave Jean the job of Transport Manager. Every other week the young people would need taking to other clubs for games and quizzes. Volunteers for this were scarce and Frank ended up driving every week, sometimes being the only chauffeur for the five-a-side football team. He did it for some time but eventually it became a chore and other people came along, allowing the couple to leave the club.

Other interests opened up. Frank and Jean attended the village church where he had spent so much time as a boy and they began to help out with various jobs. Frank did a little bell-ringing but not on a regular basis. He went on to the village hall committee and served for twenty years, being responsible for all the day-to-day maintenance jobs with help from Dan Short on any electrical problems. Jean was soon busy with the Women's Institute. But in 1971 something more unusual was added to the Stonesfield activities list: Modern Sequence Dancing.

A couple living near the war memorial, Barbara and Ron Davies, were very keen on dancing and the idea probably came from them but the group was actually started by a gentleman, Mr Percy Thompson from Woodstock. He was a teacher at Marlborough School and had taught Jean as a girl. Frank's experience of dancing was limited to a

Frank and Jean in the dancing years – at daughter Rosemary's wedding in 1984

shuffle round the floor in his army days, and then not until a few pints had given him the courage. Jean, on the other hand, had learnt to dance as a teenager in Bladon and went to lessons in Bletchingdon and Kirtlington. She persuaded Frank to join the new group and soon he was beginning to enjoy being able to dance properly.

In 1972 the first committee was formed and the club officially became known as 'Stonesfield Dance Club – Modern Sequence.' The club was very popular and members came from as far afield as Shipston on Stour and Moreton-in-Marsh, as well as the rather more local Kidlington, Botley, Witney, Woodstock, North Leigh and Charlbury areas. But out of a membership of forty or so very few people came from Stonesfield itself. At first this was not a problem, with lessons held in the village hall on Thursday evenings. Three or four times a year the club held a Saturday dance which attracted between seventy and eighty people, the final dance always being held at the end of October when the clocks were put back. Then the departing dancers were told, "Goodnight – you'll be home before you've left here!"

Frank became an accomplished dancer and was Chairman of the club for twenty years. Towards the end of this time membership began to fall. Many of the members now were elderly and found it more difficult to turn out on a winter's night and drive to Stonesfield for two hours' dancing. Dancers had joined from Headington and Abingdon and once off the A44 would get lost on the dark, unmarked country roads around the village. Club membership rose and fell, once dropping to four or five couples and then recovering slightly. Towards the end about sixteen or eighteen people kept the club going. Just six of these were from Stonesfield and the dancers were taught by Ernie Slater who by now was over ninety years old and travelling over from Ducklington. The committee decided not to wait until things petered out but to call an end to the club while it still had a reasonable membership.

The Sequence Dancing had finished but village people still had the option of Country Dancing. This had been running alongside the Stonesfield Dance Club in the village hall every Wednesday evening and still continued. Don and Ruby Strudwick were responsible for starting the Country Dance Club giving a country village another outlet for people's energy and interest.

In 1972 Aunt Edie died. The only people left in the old house were Frank's father and Edie's son. Although blind, Percy still had his allotments but with no woman in the house it was decided it would be best for him to go and live with Frank's youngest sister, Mary, over in Woodstock. He lived there until his death in 1976.

When his father moved away Frank took over the three allotments. At that time allotments were as popular as ever and people were keen to have one. Still working for Amey's, Frank found the three plots quite a handful but he worked them for about twenty years. During the 1990s he began to think he might give up one so when Mary Parsons mentioned that her husband, another Percy, was interested in having an allotment he was pleased to hand one over to him. Frank had known

Mary since she was a baby but had not met Percy who was a Wootton man. The couple had just come to live in Stonesfield but Percy was still working his two allotments at Wootton. He came down to see Frank and was very happy to take over one of the plots. It would be much more convenient to have an allotment nearer home.

The two men became good friends; if Frank mentioned that a piece of ground needed rotavating he would often find that Percy had done it for him. Although Percy still had a full-time job, the following year Frank gave him a second allotment, leaving himself with just one. Percy loved being on his allotments. His crops were second to none and he gave much of what he grew to friends and neighbours. The garden of his cottage opposite the top of Peak's Lane was given over to producing plants from seed. Heated platforms in the greenhouse produced fine specimens, many of which were destined for the village shows. He had always been a great supporter of the produce shows, usually competing against another keen grower, his brother, and he passed on a lot of his knowledge of showing to Frank. Percy had started work on the land and, like many others, had gone on to work at the car factory in Cowley before finishing up in a local garage. He was a skilled metal-worker who could make his own gardening tools.

Soon, Percy retired from his job at the garage in Milton-under-Wychwood and looked forward to spending many more pleasant hours working on his plot next to Frank, chatting and comparing and shaking their heads at the caterpillars and the weather. But Percy's retirement was quite short. During the following year he was struck down by a massive heart attack and died. Frank had lost a great friend.

20

But life goes on and soon another gardener had the privilege of taking over Percy's allotment and listening to Frank's stories. Frank was more fortunate than Percy; he had already had many years of retirement. But what is retirement? For a man like Frank it is often just a shift from paid to unpaid work. And be it putting out the church rubbish bin for collection, tidying the war memorial or giving someone

Uncle Frank's tree (2008)

a lift to the medical centre – he will do it gladly. For this is a man whose warmth and humanity are as vital to a community as is the rain that falls on the soil he has worked all his life.

Now, the bean sticks have been taken down and the last row of carrots pulled up. Uncle Frank's huge walnut tree overlooks the ground which has been turned over, ready for someone else to start work. At eighty-five years old Frank has decided to give up his allotment. After all, he still has his garden and there is plenty of room there for the greenhouse, flowers, fruit and vegetables. And with the summer shows to enter there will always be something to do……

And while he works in the garden, tends the war memorial, or most especially when he stands waiting quietly there with his wreath on Remembrance Sunday, a wartime song often comes back to him. He cannot remember who wrote it or even when he first heard it but he knows it was somewhere, sometime in Europe and he cannot forget it. It was a poignant song for some of those young soldiers who not only had to cope with the combat and harsh conditions but also with knowing that their wives and girlfriends were no longer waiting for them. Among the many names and faces that Frank will always

Sergeant Hall, Sixth Airborne, Remembrance Sunday 2008

remember training, fighting, suffering and laughing with were some in that unhappy position. And although their broken hearts were often hidden behind a joke and a pint everyone knew that this war had a lot to answer for. There is nothing like a song for bringing all those memories flooding back.

To the tune of 'Lily Marlene':

I've just come back to England from fighting overseas,
Instead of love and kisses my girl gave me the breeze.
She said she preferred the Yanks and gum, a little jeep, a country run,
My goodtime English sweetheart, my faithful English rose.

I've been away a long time with thoughts of coming home,
My heart was full of yearning for love I've never known.
But during my absence long and grim the Yanks bought you with lime and gin,
My goodtime English sweetheart, my faithful English rose.

So now I've asked the army to put me on a ship –
You think me very barmy to take another trip.
But when my lifeblood starts to flow my thoughts will go to Yanks I know,
My goodtime English sweetheart, my faithful English rose.

I suppose you will be happy when I'm dead and gone and
Other ladies' sweethearts will still be fighting on.
For this song was meant for girls like you from one like me whose love's so true,
My goodtime English sweetheart, my faithful English rose.

An Unknown Soldier,
Written during World War Two,
1939 – 1945.